Spoilt

ABOUT THE AUTHOR

Terry Denby was born in West Ham, London in 1947. After leaving school with no qualifications he became interested in music and began playing the guitar, eventually with bands in some of London's best known hotels. He later acquired an Honours degree and worked as a teacher in a school in East London. Terry now lives in France with his wife and daughter.

Spoilt

The abandoned child who had nowhere to turn
– an astonishing true story

Terry Denby

HODDER

Extract from 'Streets of London' by Ralph McTell used by kind permission of
Westminster Music Ltd.

First published in Great Britain in 2007
by Hodder & Stoughton
An Hachette Livre UK company

First published in paperback in 2008

A CIP catalogue record for this title is available from the British Library

ISBN 978 0340 91036 8

Typeset in Sabon by Avon DataSet Ltd,
Bidford on Avon, Warwickshire

Printed and bound in Great Britain by
Clays Ltd, St Ives plc

The paper used in this book is a natural recyclable product
made from wood grown in sustainable forests.
The hard coverboard is recycled.

Hodder & Stoughton Ltd
338 Euston Road
London NW1 3BH
www.hodder.co.uk

Some of the names of characters, places and institutions have been changed to protect the subjects' identity.

Contents

Prologue

The recollections that follow, the scenes in the council flat, the magistrates' court, police custody, the children's home, the tête-à-tête with the child psychologist; none of these were ever intended to report what was actually said word for word. Looking back on one's childhood is not an exact science and in the following pages I have often invented dialogue for dramatic effect where I have forgotten exactly what was said at the time. I have, nevertheless, aimed at verisimilitude and hope that, with or without the writer's bent, I have accurately described what happened.

Anyone who goes around writing books reveals secrets. For many years I kept my secret to myself, embarrassed and embittered by the turn of events on my last day at the children's home and by what was said to me at the meeting I had with the child psychologist soon afterwards. What happened to me was unspeakable, but as I have grown in self-confidence, knowing I have done nothing to be ashamed of, I have reached a stage where I am able to speak freely and openly.

I wrote this book because I want others to understand what it is like for a child to be devoid of love – indeed, devoid of any emotion; to undergo years of neglect; to become unfeeling and badly damaged.

But perhaps the bottom line is that I wrote this book because I have such a story to tell.

I

The Buildings

And lead you through the streets of London
From the song 'The Streets of London'
by Ralph McTell

1953

'Fuck Jesus.' The words came to mind as I, barely six years of age, spent the morning looking for cigarette-ends for my mother. I'd searched around outside my school and was turning into Manor Road when I found a beauty. It was long, firm and cleaner than a joke on children's television. But, above all, it still had some length left to it and was dry.

'Fuck Jesus, hardly smoked,' I muttered to myself, stooping quickly down to the pavement. I placed the dog-end in my tobacco-tin and continued along the road, eyes down.

It was a long, straight road bounded on one side by rows of council flats known as The Buildings, and on the other side by the architecturally untidy LCC (London County Council) Works Depot. There was also a railway that ran down to the docks. Beyond the railway was a power station and a dark mountain of coal.

Soon I heard a train approaching, travelling in the direction of the docks. I turned towards it and counted the wagons as they trundled by, exaggerating their number to myself. The train had a hypnotic effect on me and I began to daydream; it was the dream of a child that would have required a professional to interpret – of kings and queens in steam machines. As the last wagon of the goods train disappeared in the distance, my lungs caught some of the smoke from the puffing engine, and from this other world I suddenly came back to earth with a cough, my heart pounding. For a moment I stared at everything and nothing. Everything coughed smoke: the power station, the train.

I resumed my search, scuffing my shoes along the pavement and chafing my mind with ever more romantic thoughts. Suddenly there were rich pickings. I stooped to the pavement time and again until the tin was full. Mum would be pleased. I ran home, fair hair, hand-me-down grey jersey and short trousers, which were torn from leg to leg under the crotch and hanging from my waist like a faded kilt, all were blowing in the wind.

Home was drained of colour. A second tenement block stood in the shadow of the first, and so on; mirror copies with a uniform number of windows and doors in each block venting an aura of decay.

A curtain moved as I went into the dark entrance of The Building that was mine. I walked along the short passage, took hold of the iron railing, and climbed the stairs two at a time to the first floor. A pane of glass was missing from the front door. I approached, reached up, turned the knob of the Yale from the inside, and let myself into the flat.

I found my mother in the front room sitting at the piano, contemplating a cigarette that was burning a black stripe into the base key-block. She was seemingly at a loss as to what to play.

'Look!' I exclaimed, opening the tobacco-tin. I moved closer to her. 'Look what I've got.'

She took the tobacco-tin from me. 'Why aren't you at school?' she asked, good-humouredly.

'Got sent home.'

'What for this time?'

'Dunno, didn't do nothin'.'

'Gertcha,' she said.

My mother played a few notes, putting an emphasis on skill rather than tone. This disadvantaged her, since skill is widespread but art is contained. And then suddenly she got angry:

'Tell the teachers they're not to send you home next time. Who do they think we are?' She was raising her voice – again. She resented interference from teachers. If it weren't for the school inspector endlessly chasing her up, I don't suppose she would have sent me at all. She regularly had discussions with the school inspector on the threshold of the front door. Time and again she made excuses for my behaviour and her own negligence.

Fishy came in from the bedroom and went over to the stove, awoken by the urgency in my mother's voice. There was no 'good morning' or any other kind of greeting. That would have been considered sissy. Fishy was my mother's private name for the man. He was a window-cleaner. In his late thirties, he looked as if he'd been sleeping rough on Wanstead Flats for three nights. Thin and puckered, he appeared as though every day of his life something had been taken from him, and nothing given in return except the breath to breathe. Simply existing was almost more than he could manage. He was short and had a crooked nose. What were left of his teeth were uneven and yellowed like the piano keys and his eyes were bloodshot, his face unshaven.

The stove was out, but Fishy turned his back on it anyway

and started rubbing his buttocks. Slowly, with scraggy fingers, he massaged his stiff muscles with precision.

My mother had begun to extract the tobacco from the dog-ends. She dropped the loose tobacco back into the tin, then dropped the paper on to the bass key-block of the piano. Later she would roll the tobacco into new fags.

'Bit early, innit, for the old Joanna?' Fishy asked.

My mother continued with the task of unpacking the tobacco.

'Give us "We'll Meet Again", Emily,' said Fishy, wondering, I suppose, if he'd hurt my mother's feelings.

She stopped what she was doing and brandished her hands over the keys. The piano had ready-made notes, of course, and if she was lucky enough to strike the correct keys at near enough the right time, and prudent enough to stay in the key of C or C sharp – that is to say, either on the black notes or on the white notes, but never black and white together – then she could derive some pleasure from playing a simple melody over a bass accompaniment. Chords or discords, depending upon how her luck was running, were introduced as opportunities presented themselves and something approaching harmonic structure and body was given to whatever tune was being attacked. This element of luck suited my mother's personality. Her playing technique was unorthodox, and she had not changed or tried to improve it one iota in my living memory.

This particular morning the top of the piano was open and the front had been removed to expose the workings and accentuate the instrument's fashionable honky-tonk sound. Fishy and I watched and listened. My mother's left hand put me in mind of a pumping action, first a bass note, and then a chord several tones higher; she seemed to *pump* the notes out of the instrument. I was fascinated by the action of the hammers as they fluttered against the strings like untamed birds in a cage. Fishy began to sing along with plenty of vibrato in his voice.

My mother stopped suddenly on a cadence that sounded interrupted, took her cigarette from the base key-block, and sucked some life into it.

I loved her dark hair, which was combed in a large tsunami on top of her head. Above all, I loved the way she let me get away with murder. She had her dark moods, but they were always short and sharp, nothing to take my thumb out of my mouth for. She looked down in a dream at the yellowed keys and started to play again that jewel of a song that was already so familiar to my ears. Fishy tapped his foot on the lino in time to the music. With a child's lack of reason, I danced my way around the room.

There was never enough food in the flat, just scraps of this and that. I don't ever remember feeling particularly hungry (I always managed to get hold of some sweets, which numbed my appetite), but I remember the food cupboard in the scullery was always bare. Refrigerators were unheard of in our part of London at the time, so food had to be kept in a cupboard – and it wasn't a good idea to keep it there for too long. Crickets and spiders would find their way in, and it wasn't unusual to find a rat climbing over some long-forgotten morsel. I was often sent out to buy fish and chips, which were cheap and needed no storage, preparation or cooking. My mother would take her purse from where it was hidden in the back-hollow of the piano.

'Go and get some Lilian Gish. And get some for him as well,' she would add as an afterthought, nodding in Fishy's direction. 'And do your Uncle Bert up, for fuck's sake, and put your weasel on.' I was initiated into the closed world of rhyming

Cockney slang from birth. We used it to outwit authority and eavesdroppers, but it spilled over into all aspects of our lives.

I would return home from the fish and chip shop not only with Lilian Gish and chips, but also with Harvey Nichols (pickles) and three or four large gherkins which my mother called 'wallies'. The meal was eaten straight out of the linen draper (newspaper) that it was wrapped in. I would close the fall of the Joanna (piano) and eat mine from there, while my mother and Fishy were seated on the settee. They never had meals up at the table for the curious reason that they would have regarded that as being too much like conforming to the established order of the middle and upper classes.

As they ate their fish and chips they would read the linen that it was wrapped in. I remember Fishy tilting his head sideways once to look at an account of the preparations for the Everest expedition. 'Catch me going up bloomin' mountains this weather!' he exclaimed. 'Top of my ladder is high enough for me, and cold enough, fank you.' And then, clearing his throat: 'I wonder what makes a bloke do that sort of thing?'

'Bees and honey,' said my mother. 'That Sir John 'unt fella's got a few bob. I bet you he's seen some life.'

If I wasn't running errands, I was forever being told to go back to school or to play outside and I would find myself on the street thinking about what I could get up to.

Apart from Fishy, there were others who visited us. There was Curly, a lost sailor, and Chris, a cabinet maker. Chris used to come along the road smelling of exotic wood. It wasn't offensive; on the contrary, it was fragrant. And then there was Raymond, a red-haired Irishman who was interested in human biology in an academic sense and told us about the functions of vitamins. Fishy said very little. He wasn't a talker, he was a thinker. I liked that, but of course I never quite knew what he was thinking. I learned later that he had had a contract with the LCC at the time.

The council's requirement for the cleaning of the windows in its buildings must have been enormous. To begin with, there were the schools; then there was the Italian Renaissance town hall with its over-generous fenestrations; the libraries, the public baths; the museum; the college of further education. Fishy wouldn't have achieved very much on his own with one small, wooden ladder, but I guess his services were needed for the occasional small job.

He was an unprincipled sort of man. Because he had so little, he resented other people having so much. His rule for life was the kind that is born out of resentment, and his social standing was such that, even from the top of his ladder, I don't think he had anybody to look down on, except me.

It was early evening when, dirty and bored, I went back indoors. My mother and Fishy were still in the front room, half-asleep and half-dressed.

With nothing better to do, I looked out through the closed window. There were clouds rising over the rooftops and I detected a chill in the air. Fishy, as if reading my mind, got out of his armchair and placed the palm of his hand over the hotplate of the stove, as if he needed reminding that it was cold and there was no flame flickering inside. He screwed up some of the newspaper from the fish and chips into several tight balls and used them as firelighters under some sticks of wood and a few pieces of coke. These were the days when coke was not a drink or a drug, but a solid fuel. We felt the need for a fire. It was cold and we had been talking about Everest. What was left of the newspaper would be saved and later torn into squares and put on the shelf in the lavatory. We never had proper toilet paper, not even as a treat; that would have been too bourgeois, I suppose.

As the flames in the stove took hold, my mother went into the scullery and made another pot of tea. I liked mine milky, with heaps of sugar. She brought it into the front room and, as I drank, I watched my mother apply varnish to her fingernails.

'You going out?' I asked.

'Yup, we're going to the Angel.' She took something flat from her handbag, unscrewed the top, and a small mirror popped up. She studied her reflection for a long second, wet a tiny brush with the tip of her tongue, and slowly and carefully spread cream on to her eyelashes and brows.

'Can I come?'

'Tch, tch.'

She put her mascara away and went over to the wall mirror, turned her head to one side and then to the other. Then she held out her hands in front of her and studied them. They were a little shaky.

'Don't act stupid, boy,' she said, looking at my reflection in the mirror. 'You know you're not allowed in the rub-a-dub-dub.'

I suppose it would have been about half-past seven when Fishy took a poker to the stove and made it safe before opening the front door. My mother told me to stay put, but I darted along the passage and downstairs ahead of them.

Fishy's car was parked in the road. It was black with two doors and a sun roof. He settled himself in the driver's seat and tried to start the engine, leaving my mother to fend for herself. She must have rather fancied she was the cock of the walk as she opened the door on her side and stepped on to the running-board. I nipped in before her, on to the back seat. The smell of leather reminded me of a police car. I pressed my nose hard up against the seat in front of me. My mother struck a pose for the benefit of the neighbours, whom she must have known were watching from behind drawn curtains, and then sat down next to Fishy.

He was having difficulty in starting the engine as usual, but eventually it fired and we drove past our Building, through the back streets and over the mini-roundabout with the lamp-post in the middle. Pulling out on to the main road again, we weaved our way through the late-evening traffic until, after a mile or two, Fishy stopped the car. We were outside a sweetshop. My mother took her ration book and a sixpence from her purse.

'Take these and buy some sweets.' She stepped on to the running-board to let me out.

'No,' I said, cowering in the back seat. 'You'll drive off.'

'Tch, don't act so stupid, boy.' She turned to Fishy. 'You're not going to drive off without Terry, are you?'

''Course not,' he said. He took another sixpence from his trouser pocket.

I accepted the money, but my bottom lip trembled and I wrestled to hold back a flood of tears. Giving my mother a spiteful look, I got out of the car. She sat down again quickly, pulled the door to and, before I could demur further, Fishy let the clutch in and drew away from the kerb.

I watched the car disappear down the road and then turned towards the sweetshop and began to weigh up my options. I knew how comforting chocolate could be. It would ease the lump in my throat and the heaviness in my chest. As the chocolate dissolved in my mouth, my troubles would melt away with it. But I also needed the bus or train fare home and I wasn't sure how much that would cost out of my shilling. So I stood outside the sweetshop in a dilemma. Should I go home on a bus or a train chocolate-less, or should I spend the money on chocolate and then walk home? At my time of life I didn't feel that I could deal with such unwelcome alternatives. It was getting dark. One way or another I had to decide fairly soon.

The shopkeeper came out of the shop and began closing up for the night, placing a metal guard in front of the plate-glass window. We both looked up at the rain-filled sky. I looked down again and sighed. Then, licking my lips, I went into the shop and, when the shopkeeper came back in, I bought some sweet and sugary things that cost the whole 1/-.

I started to walk home. I didn't have the faintest idea where I was, but with a lost-dog instinct I knew I was heading in the right direction. The houses were tall, foreboding, all huddled together and leaning to support one another. Further on, the outlines of the tall buildings were replaced by the low, rounded profiles of Nissen huts on either side of the road. There were lights in the windows that cast a glow across the pavement. Bow Bells struck a jumble of faint harmonics and I filled my mouth with chocolate. It tasted good. Life wasn't so bad. But to the passer-by in the street I must have looked a sorry sight.

It was raining as I went past West Ham Underground station, so I went inside to shelter, found a corner and, like a beardless tramp, lay down and fell fast asleep.

The next thing I heard was the rumble of a train in the distance, the rhythmic, allargando beat of the wheels as they passed over the rails, proof of its dying momentum.

And then I heard a voice: 'Is there another Way Out?'

I opened my eyes. A policeman was questioning the ticket-collector, a short, underfed Cockney with hollow eyes and sunken cheeks.

'No, there's no other Way Out,' the ticket-collector confirmed.

'Let's see if the boy's mother is on this train,' said the policeman. 'If she isn't, I'll walk the lad home.'

They took up their positions at the barrier and, in ones and twos, the passengers came into view at the top of the stairs. In the lead was an elderly man who passed through without noticing anybody, then, in quick succession, two soldiers in uniform, a local villain, who I recognised, and suddenly all was quiet again.

The policeman looked at me and shook his head. 'Come on, Terry,' he said. 'Time to go home. You can't stay here all bloomin' night.'

'Do you know the lad, then?' asked the ticket-collector.

Without answering, the policeman took me by the hand and walked me past another silent vagrant who was standing at the entrance to the station, a variant outcast a generation ahead of me. Rain blew in through the open entrance and was blotted up by the porous concrete floor to within a few inches of the tramp's restless feet. He stared at us, found his voice, and began singing: 'I really can't stay, I've got to go 'way'. He couldn't have been a day over thirty, but it looked to me as if there were an old man behind the unkempt beard. The policeman looked the other way and, when the rain eased, led me safely out into the gas-lit road.

We reached The Buildings quickly, ran across the mini-roundabout with the lamp-post in the middle, and eventually into the dark entrance of The Building that I called home. As we climbed the stairs, the moon showed its face from behind a cloud and sulked through the rusting metal grill that was cemented into the wall at the end of the landing.

There was a light burning behind the neighbour's front door. The policeman was about to knock when the door was opened from the inside. A familiar nauseating smell came from within.

'G'mornin', Mrs Richardson,' said the policeman to the half-starved woman who stood on the threshold. 'You any idea where Mrs Denby is?'

'She went out about seven o'clock last night.' The neighbour touched her chin with two fingers and a thumb and looked at me. 'Ain't seen her since.' She leaned backwards clumsily to glance at the clock on her kitchen table. 'Gone one o'clock.'

'I'll let the lad in, then.' The policeman put his hand through the broken pane of glass and turned the knob of the Yale. A rat scuttled away and a dozen panic-stricken cockroaches reinstated themselves under the floorboards as he found the light switch. 'I'm sure your mum will be home soon,' he said, ushering me inside.

'It's terrible,' I heard Mrs Richardson say. She was still waiting on the threshold of her front door. 'He's disadvantaged, that one, from having too many men around the house.'

The policeman obviously wasn't in the mood to respond to her rhetoric. He was already making his way down the stairs, and the sound of his footsteps was echoing around the stairwell.

I took my wet clothes off, got into bed, and lay down quite still with the lights on while something scratched in a corner.

A detailed report about the events must have found its way to the powers that be because soon afterwards a person from the LCC came to see us. My mother was out, but a man of middle age (he looked Neanderthal to me) knocked at the front door so persistently that I let him in. He questioned me, and then went next door and gleaned some more useful information about my situation from Mrs Richardson.

'You wouldn't Adam and Eve it,' she said. She seemed only too pleased to stand outside her front door and tell all. According to her, there were parties that went on all night and visitors all day. I stood on the landing listening to Mrs Richardson's evocative words and phrases: 'neglected', 'filthy', 'sight for sore eyes', 'swears like a trooper'.

'I've spoken to the boy's headmaster at school,' responded the man from the LCC. 'Absenteeism, riotous behaviour, bullying, learning difficulties, lack of progress, have all been confirmed.' Before he left I heard him say to Mrs Richardson that I was on his list of children at risk, and that this latest occurrence was 'the last straw'. I wondered what he meant.

My mother's own words were self-damning. The LCC had contacted her, inviting her to go along to the office, for a chat. I went with her and she told them flatly what a handful I was and how she couldn't manage. We were seated on straight-backed chairs, and across the desk I faced the same man who had come to visit me before, my boy-sized body swallowed up by the room.

'. . . and his language!' my mother exclaimed. 'I don't know *where* he gets it from, honestly, I don't know where he gets it from.'

'You swear as well,' I said, looking at her.

She kicked me under the desk, and out of the side of her mouth told me to shut up.

The man behind the desk made a note of this. Evidence was being collated, that's what it was, evidence, to be presented in court before a bench of magistrates. No doubt the LCC was busy comparing records, reports and other little pieces of information until a picture emerged of what was going on. The evidence must have been pretty conclusive and my mischief well-documented.

My teachers at school called me a 'troubled child'. My peers at school called me a number of derogatory names and I was unable to get through a day without a fight with one or other of them. There was no love lost between my half-brothers and me.

My mother had said I was unmanageable. The neighbours

called me a 'little bleeder', and sometimes felt obliged to call the police for their own protection and for the protection of their property. I had broken the windows of a number of flats in Hollins Avenue, Memorial Avenue and Manor Road, spread dogs' excrement over dogs to whom it did not belong, pulled washing that was hung out to dry off its lines and run off with the pegs, and I had been caught stealing from shops no less than eight times in as many months. I had beaten up a five-year-old girl, stolen a bottle of Tizer from a parked lorry, broken into a car, and possibly committed one or two other crimes that went undocumented and that I have deliberately eradicated from my memory.

A social worker called me a 'spoilt brat' one afternoon at the child welfare department when I was summoned there. She didn't seem to think for a minute that my attention-seeking behaviour was an attempt to be loved by my mother. And a doctor prescribed tranquillisers and suggested I shouldn't eat so much sugar: I was obviously hyperactive because of a chemical imbalance.

At the time I didn't think my behaviour was that bad, but everybody must have been at their wits' end, and lending each other support to have me taken away. More and more replies to letters were no doubt received at the child welfare department from the police and from my school until at last a summons for me to appear in court arrived at the flat by post.

I was alone in the front room banging the piano keys with both hands. My mother was in bed. The noise must have been torturous for her and for the neighbours. We were surrounded by them, above, below, and on either side.

When she heard the postman's persistent knocking, my mother finally submitted and got out of bed. Her emotions must have been mixed, to say the least, as she signed for, and opened, the important-looking envelope: frustration, anger, worry, resentment. Perhaps in a way she was relieved?

She came into the front room and slammed the fall of the piano without taking her eyes off the letter. I took my hands away in the nick of time. I could see that she was having great difficulty in finding her way through what, after all, would have been legal jargon.

But it transpired, after a long discussion with a wise man who lived in the block of flats opposite us, that her right to attend the hearing was limited to her being a person directly concerned in the case – a concession, not a right. And although legal aid existed for me to be represented by a solicitor, there was no provision for my mother to be so represented.

'Now there's a fine state of affairs,' my mother said, coming back into the front room and switching on the wireless set, a cigarette bobbing up and down between her lips as she spoke. 'You've got to go to court and I don't have the right to be there. Well, I shall go to the poxy hearing whether I have the right to be there or not and give them a piece of my mind.'

She pondered the letter some more while the wireless set was delivering the news: calls were being made for a review of another court hearing, the Timothy Evans case. Although I was too young to understand the particulars, 10 Rillington Place is an address that has always remained in my mind since childhood.

Our situation was not a matter of life and death, but my mother seemed to be becoming increasingly worried and I remember there were further outbursts of unparliamentary language. Sometimes she would go on and on at the top of her voice, dealing with her frustration or whatever it was in the only way she knew how.

'Why is it that it's always people like us who are put upon?

It's not only the child welfare department, it's the fucking lot of them, the poxy government, Sir Winston Churchill, the old codger – he's seventy if he's a day – and his ministers, elderly relics; Lord this and Lord that, aristocratic independent Alphonses who haven't a clue what it's like not to have two ha'pennies to rub together. The country is looking forward to a New Elizabethan Age? [We'd heard this on the wireless set, too.] I'm not looking forward to a New Elizabethan Age. And . . . what was it he said? Hope for national recovery and glory? I'm not looking forward to anything like it. I'd like to know where the next shilling's coming from so I can feed the fucking gas and electricity meters or purchase some of this newly de-rationed food.'

Everybody round The Buildings had electricity and gas meters installed because we couldn't afford to pay the bills when they arrived. The meters recorded the amount of electricity and gas supplied to each flat. The irony was that if the gas and electricity was metered, it worked out more expensive.

The large, grey meters with complex dials and rusty-red metal pipes leading in and out of them like pulmonary veins were our piggy banks. If my mother or any of my half-brothers or half-sisters wanted some ready cash, they would pick the locks with a hairpin or just whack the meters open with a hammer and help themselves to whatever happened to be inside. I soon learned how to do it and, to this day, I'm quite handy with a hairpin or a short length of wire. But now I only pick locks to show off. Honest.

The memory of how central those gas and electricity meters were to our miserable lives amazes me even now. They were the safety net suspended beneath our day-to-day existence. When the man from the London Electricity Board or the Gas Board came to empty the meters, we remained perfectly quiet and still in the front room pretending not to be at home, listening breathlessly to the knocks at the front door and waiting for the meter man to get fed up with waiting and go away, believing that nobody was in.

My mother went over to the high mantelpiece above the stove, took down a calendar that was sitting there, and ran a nicotine-stained finger down to the date of the court hearing.

'Exactly two weeks' time,' she said, replacing the calendar.

I followed her into the scullery and helped her make a pot of tea. She loved her cuppa. She took her tea into the front room, sipping it cautiously because it was hot. Then she tilted the cup and poured some into the saucer and sipped it from there, making a slurping noise. She rolled another cigarette and lit it before opening the fall of the piano and sitting down.

It was the middle of the week and she was already looking forward to the weekend and the chance of earning some money playing the piano in the local pub. She struck a chord, a strange harmony emerged, and she began to sing along.

Then she made herself up again, plucking her eyebrows and painting her face. She looked unscrubbed but glamorous, the glamour clinging to her, like the smell of Player's Weights in a powder-puff. She told me that if I got fed up on my own, I was to go to Mavis's, my half-sister, who lived in a Nissen hut in Bow.

I was given the bus fare to get there and my mother then left me in the front room, trying to make sense of the piano keyboard and nodding my head compliantly with her commands. 'Remind me to get me weasel from Uncle's, tomorrow,' she called along the passage. I watched from an open window as she made her way along the road. Her hands were thrust deep into the pockets of her jacket and she was wearing a headscarf and squinting into a faint wind.

I wondered if Fishy would be at the pub. My mother always claimed he brought her luck. (I can see him even now, sitting at the bar in blue overalls that were spotted with everything that comes off windows, his hair slicked over the side of his head in a last-ditch attempt to look presentable.)

Moving away from the window, I looked round the flat. It was a mess. Clothes were strewn around the floor, drawers were left open, and bits of smelly food left on the table. The house flies must have thought they'd died and gone to heaven when they flew in through our window. It was just as well we were on the first floor, high enough so that people couldn't see in through the windows.

I stood in the middle of the room for a moment wondering what I could get up to. My mother might have been wondering what I was going to get up to as well. She understood that I was not just disobedient; I had the Devil in me. A day or two before in Memorial Avenue I'd seen a pram with a baby in it parked outside the butcher's. I had let the brake off and pushed it out into the road. Before that, I'd taken some children up to the Northern Outfall Sewer and encouraged them to walk along the embankment. I'd then gone off and left them where they might have fallen in and drowned. These were four- and five-year-olds! My mother knew better than anybody that this wasn't just naughtiness, it was devilry.

It was getting dark. I stood on a chair, closed the window, and decided to drop in on my half-sister, Mavis.

On leaving the flat I met a cat on the stairs, a young tabby. It was tame and looking for company. It approached me and rubbed its neck against my bare leg. I indulged the animal for a minute then picked it up by the scruff of the neck, crossed the landing, and at arm's length dropped it down the stairwell.

The animal fell with a cry to the concrete floor below. I

gloated from my vantage point as the kitten unsteadily began to orient itself, and I made my way down the stairs as it finally managed to stand on all fours. A red bubble of blood and air leaked from its mouth, grew larger, and burst silently around its lips like thin chewing-gum. I picked the cat up and returned to the top of the landing.

I'm not proud of this episode with the cat and the memory haunts me to this day, but I've included it here if only to try and show what can go on inside a child's mind when he or she feels as abandoned and unwanted as I did. My emotions were so intense at times that they manifested themselves into physical pain; my chest became constricted and my throat ached.

The next time my mother and Fishy went to the pub, I made sure I went with them. They made themselves comfortable on stools at the bar while I played outside in the road. Every so often I would push one of the heavy saloon bar doors open a little to peep inside. A telling-off from an adult was inevitable: 'Gertcha!' But that didn't deter me for long.

The colour of the ornate ceiling was nicotine-brown and it seemed to press down on me in spite of, or perhaps because of, my size. I was so small. Everything about the public house was man-size: the walls, the floor, the upright piano in the corner that looked as if it were at death's door with its broken, black and yellow, teeth-like keys and wonky fall.

I watched as drinks arrived for my mother and Fishy, and then I moved away from the doors again as people began to arrive in greater numbers.

I woke up mid-morning and lay still for a few minutes, thinking my mother liked Fishy more than any other of her men. Her voice stemmed my thoughts:

'Oi! By the way.'

I could hear her interrogating Fishy in the other bedroom.

'I meant to ask. What happened to you last Wednesday? I wanted you to drive me to the welfare centre. I prefer it when you're there. They feel sorry for me.' I heard the click of a cigarette lighter and then the indescribable reek of Old Holborn made inroads into my bedroom.

Then I became aware of the enormous clatter in the scullery as Jimmy, one of my half-brothers, prepared his breakfast of bread and dripping. He was a merchant seaman on leave, a stoker on a steamer. Twenty years old and as strong as a bull. That was his nickname – the Bull. Nobody dared argue with him, except my mother, of course.

I got out of bed and went into the scullery. My mother joined us. The gas oven was lit and serving as a heater, and we enjoyed its warmth as we helped ourselves to tea. My mother took a cup of tea to Fishy in bed. A cup and saucer and a teaspoon, though the tea was already stirred. Pure etiquette. My mother still found time for affectation. I followed her into the bedroom to get a look at him.

She placed the cup of tea on the table by the bed and he sat up and turned on the wireless set. Football. Possibly West Ham United. I don't remember who was in the squad that season, 1953, but the name 'Adey' was always on the tip of Fishy's tongue, a moniker that has stuck in my mind since childhood. Or it might have been Blackpool on the wireless set; they were headline news. Blackpool won the FA Cup Final that year against Bolton Wanderers at the old Empire Wembley Stadium, helped by the 'wizard of dribble', Stanley Matthews.

Whoever it was playing, we left Fishy to listen to the football and returned to the scullery. Jimmy was pondering his own botherations privately as he stood in front of the oven and blew cigarette smoke over the tops of our heads. Our mother fretted irritably as she placed her cup back on to its saucer and swallowed a mouthful of hot tea. I think the approaching court hearing made her especially touchy.

It was the following weekend that we had enough money to retrieve my mother's coat from the pawnbroker. My mother and I made our way across the Memorial Grounds to the trolleybus stop, held hands, and waited in the queue. In my free hand I held my toy aeroplane, and with it I Pearl Harbor'd everybody in striking distance.

The trolleybus arrived and we sat on the upper deck, or *outside* as they used to say. It was a tu'penny ha'penny ride and the bus soon stopped conveniently outside the shop in Stratford Broadway. Uncle – that is to say, the pawnbroker – seemed surprised to find himself handing my mother's coat back to her. I'm sure he thought someone must have died in the family.

'Everything OK, Emily?' he asked my mother, as he took his money.

'Why shouldn't everything be OK?' My mother was not looking at the pawnbroker, but inspecting her coat, holding it up in front of her with both hands, looking from collar to hem and to collar again.

She also retrieved her iron because she wanted to press a blouse.

Preparations were complete and, without knowing it, we returned to The Buildings to spend what was to be our last weekend together for many years.

2

Garden Gates

It was a bright morning and, to add to it, someone had wound coloured paper round the metal bars of the grills on the landings of the flats and hung out balloons. The monarchists were getting ready for the coming coronation of Queen Elizabeth II. Having those rusty grills decorated made such a difference to the look of the place, and as my mother and I went downstairs and out into the road, for once we took a bright impression with us.

We took the trolleybus to Stratford. After a short walk along the Broadway, my mother led me up some steps and into the courthouse through a set of huge double doors. They were intimidating – even bigger and more intimidating than the doors of the pub.

To our left was a wide staircase that led up to the courtrooms and already there were people milling around at the top, their voices echoing around the high-ceilinged building. One or two people paced up and down, chain-smoking. Others were sitting on benches, studying official-looking documents and conversing in undertones. Policemen in uniform waited confidently. My mother looked unequal to them in her not-quite-long-enough brown coat. She was about to show my summons to one of them and ask directions when she was approached by an usher and we were directed upstairs to a waiting room.

'The boy's case is to be heard in the courtroom to the right,' the usher shouted after us. 'Make sure you're ready.' It was an order, not a request.

I'd been feeling edgy for some time and I turned and ran back down the stairs, heading for the double doors and the busy main road beyond. I went headlong into the outstretched arms of a policeman. Without flinching or interrupting his stride, or even so much as an *'ello, what have we got here, then?*, he lifted me off the floor and brought me back to the bottom of the staircase. I gripped the balustrade with one hand, my aeroplane with the other, and refused to let go of either.

The usher shifted his gaze. 'Are you the boy's mother?'

'Yerst. I can't do a thing with him.' She wagged a finger at me menacingly, undid my hand from the balustrade, and led me upstairs again to the waiting room while the policeman and the usher closed ranks at the bottom.

A number of people were sitting in the waiting room, talking in the common thief's greasy vernacular. I landed my aeroplane, took hold of both lapels of my jacket, and adjusted the collar with a sharp flick of the wrists before sitting down next to them. My mother lit a cigarette, nervously blew smoke in all directions, and watched as some of it curled towards the ceiling.

There was no fun to be had, so while she was distracted I returned to the top of the stairs and looked over the balcony.

I recognised the policeman waiting downstairs, arms akimbo. He was the one who had walked me home from the Underground station. He was talking to the man and lady from the child welfare department, but there was someone with them I hadn't seen before. I went downstairs to get a better look and crept up behind them.

They were all looking at some papers and absorbed in what they were reading. The person I didn't recognise, I soon discovered, was the solicitor acting for the LCC.

I don't know what they were reading exactly, but at the time family law was very complex and there was a whole series of statutes that regulated the reception of children into care. An action would have been brought against me, as being a child in need of care and protection. The solicitor would have had the choice of implementing the 1948 Children's Act, or alternatively, the Children's and Young Persons' Act 1933 which replaced Petty Sessions.

The 1948 Children's Act accounted for the majority of children coming into care at the time, about 70 per cent. It imposed a duty on the local authority to receive a child into care and gave them the discretion to vest parental rights and privileges in themselves where it appeared that the child was under seventeen years of age, had no parents or guardian, or had been abandoned, or was lost, or his parents or guardian were not providing for his proper accommodation, maintenance and upbringing.

I've since been advised that the *duty* under the 1948 Children's Act is a passive duty; only to *receive* – and that in my case the magistrates could have been acting *ultra vires* by making out a care order under this section; that is to say, acting beyond the power and outside the definition of the law as it stood.

That's jargon to me, but what is clear is that at the time over 100,000 delinquents were juveniles or young offenders and the aim of the courts was to cure rather than to punish.

The Children's and Young Persons' Act 1933 may have provided some safer options. The court could have decided, for example, that my mother was unfit to look after me or that she was not exercising proper care and guardianship. Or they could have decided that I was falling into bad associations, was beyond control, or exposed to moral danger. All of these conditions were provided for under section 61 of the Act and the magistrates only needed to be satisfied that one of them existed before making out an order.

The usher called and my mother came looking for me. My days of running amok, for the time being at least, were numbered.

The courtroom was light and airy with a high vaulted ceiling and carved-oak wall-panelling to the height of my shoulders. The three magistrates, two men and a woman, were seated on a raised plinth facing another set of those huge double doors. They all wore reading glasses and were peering over the rims at us as we entered. The solicitor sat down to the right of the bench of magistrates, alone, because he was the only legal representative present. Opposite him were the empty rows of public benches, and next to these were seats for social workers and other officials.

The policeman sat down with the man and woman from the child welfare department. The clerk to the justices sat directly in front of the magistrates, but on the lower level. To the clerk's extreme right the usher stood in a little boxed-off area, and my mother and I stood facing the magistrates.

They appeared thrown by my young age. I was six years old, obviously too young to understand what was going on and there was nobody to represent either me or my mother.

'Are you the boy's mother?' the clerk asked in an unpleasant, unconversational tone.

'Yerst,' she said.

The chairman leaned forward. 'What did she say?'

'She's the boy's mother, Your Worship.' The clerk turned to my mother again. 'Your son, Mrs Denby, has been summoned here this morning because an action has been brought against him by the London County Council who believes him to be beyond control and in need of care and protection.'

'Yerst,' she replied.

'Are you being assisted, Mrs Denby?'

My mother seemed to have lost her voice.

'Sit down,' said the clerk. 'Not there, *there*.' He pointed to the public benches and she sat down opposite the solicitor.

The clerk turned his attention to me. 'Do you understand that we are not here to punish you? We are here to help. If anybody says anything to you, will you speak up? The magistrates must hear what you have to say for yourself.'

I wiped my nose with the lower part of my sleeve. Then, looking up at the ceiling, I threw my aeroplane into the air and Pearl Harbor'd the lot of them.

The enormous, polished door-knob slid through my small hands as I tried to turn it one way and then the other. This was going to be a hard landing. The usher hurried across. I took a swipe at his spectacles and sent them flying. The chairman of the bench stood up and ineffectually said how absurdly inappropriate this was, or something equally ridiculous. He was a slight man, but his expression, as he surveyed the scene with evident dislike, suggested he could be a hard sentencer.

'Fetch a policeman,' shouted the female magistrate.

The policeman who had walked me home from the Underground station hesitated and then stood up with some apparent misgivings. I suppose he thought he was having a day off.

My mother remained seated, nervously biting the ends of the fingers of one hand, but the lady from the child welfare department was on her feet with her wits about her, and she grabbed me by the arm and tried to restrain me. My flaying arms and legs must have been a blur. I laid into her and we rolled on the floor in front of the magistrates. I was used to fighting. I used my hands, feet, head and mouth. 'You cunt,' I said, before sinking my teeth into her hand, drawing blood. I easily had the better of her. I continued to bite her until two policemen rushed into the courtroom, put a full nelson on me, and hauled me in front of the magistrates again. Both dicks were kneeling awkwardly on the floor, each restraining one of my arms.

I continued to struggle so the chairman of the bench ordered me to be removed from the courtroom. My mother was turfed out with me and, with the two policemen standing behind keeping guard, I watched the proceedings unfold through the crack between the double doors, which to me at the time seemed like a huge gap.

I remember seeing the solicitor get to his feet, and I suppose he might have explained to the magistrates that he meant to call evidence to prove that conditions of the Children's and Young Persons' Act 1933, section 61, paragraph 1(a), were not in fact being met in respect of me and that I was being deprived of, and was in need of, the care and protection that the 1933 Act provided for.

If he had any feeling for his vocation at all, the solicitor would have told the magistrates about the miserable circumstances and conditions that surrounded me and the unhappy associations that I was falling into, being left to wander the streets on my own half the night until my mother decided to come home from the pub. He could quite truthfully have described our flat as being an excuse for a home, shared with rats, crickets, cockroaches, lice and other parasitic insects that infested the walls, floors, cupboards and bedding. He could have reasonably argued that the wallpaper was falling off in strips, that the bedrooms were bare of furniture, and the floors sticky with grime. He might have indicated that my mother's interests were outside and away from the home, using the word 'home' loosely, and he should at the very least have produced medical records showing that I had had pneumonia and suffered from epileptic fits.

He might even have obtained written evidence from my primary school showing that on those rare occasions when I attended, I disrupted lessons, damaged equipment, bullied other children and threw lighted matches down the fronts of the girls' gymslips.

Surely he must have told them about my dishevelled appearance and how it had a detrimental effect on the whole school, and how the parents of other children were warning them to stay away from me (I sometimes went to school without socks on and with holes in my shoes, and frequently had to be sent home to wash because I was so filthy).

The solicitor might well have produced a letter from the manager of the LCC Maintenance Department who was responsible for repairing the damage I caused at school and to other council property, the Memorial Grounds, West Ham Park, the streets themselves. (Breaking windows was one of my favourite pastimes. I loved the sound of splintering glass and the excitement of the chase that followed. I was too fast for any of them and had the element of surprise on my side.)

The chairman of the bench was thinking hard, considering maybe sanctioning a suitable punishment for me in the interests of justice and law and order. Refusing to restrain a bully with lighted matches in the playground was, after all, only one step away from refusing to arrest an armed robber as he shot his way out of a bank.

As a team, the magistrates glanced down at the evidence that was before them. One of the policemen who was waiting outside the courtroom with us finally tut-tutted, pulled me away from the double doors, and told me not to be so nosy. It was fortuitous that he did because at that moment the usher pushed open one of the doors from the inside.

I heard the chairman of the bench ask if there were any further questions. He was looking round at his panel, his rapid glance clearly suggesting that he would rather like it if they had none. 'OK,' he said. 'Let's have the boy and his mother back and then perhaps we can listen to what the constable has to say.'

Flanked by the two policemen, I was brought before the magistrates again. My mother sat down again on the public bench.

'Now look here,' said the chairman. 'Behave yourself properly, like a big boy, and I will allow you to sit with your mother during these proceedings. Will you also promise me that if anybody asks you a question you will answer, truthfully?'

I shrugged my shoulders and sat down next to my mother.

'Mrs Denby,' said the chairman. 'Do you have any questions?'

'What about?'

'Stand up when you speak.'

She got to her feet in confusion.

'Anything at all,' he said.

'No,' she said, and sat down again.

The police constable was asked to step forward and the solicitor got to his feet to question him.

'I believe you are the kind of officer,' he began, smoothly, 'who would rather keep a threepenny bit inside his glove and clip a young offender round the ear, no matter how big and brawny he might be, instead of running him in for some minor misdeed, providing of course that the juvenile was not a habitual wrongdoer?'

'Yes, sir, that's right. I might add that a ticking off, preferably in front of the parents, often does a great deal of good. As soon as whatever the youngster has been up to is brought out into the open, it seems to jolt some sense into the whole family. As well as policing, I see my job as liaising between family members to try and bring about some mutual understanding.'

The chairman's right-hand man narrowed his eyes and nodded to indicate admiration. 'Are you well acquainted with this boy?' he asked. 'And have you tried to liaise between him and his mother?'

'Yes, sir.'

'You had any degree of success?'

'No, sir. I think it's a bit late in the day for liaising. He needs discipline, a father with a firm hand. I've done all I could, but it's hopeless. Got to recognise facts. A child's motives for behaving in a delinquent manner vary. In Terry we have a rebel who is seeking attention because of the indifference the world is showing him. His offences may appear trivial, but they are the first steps on a ladder that can lead to serious crime.'

'Tell us about some of the things the boy gets up to.'

'Pulling washing off lines, for a start, things like that. Smashing windows . . .'

'To gain entry?'

'No, I don't think it's that. He's just got the Devil inside him.'

The policeman was asked to take his seat and it was the turn of the lady from the child welfare department to do all she could to have me put away. She was recovering from the roughing up I'd given her, but still red in the face as she stepped forward.

She read from a prepared statement, something about the importance of me being removed from my present environment before it was too late to reverse familiar trends that were developing. 'In one of our new local authority children's homes,' she ended, 'he will receive the understanding and attention that he needs.' She was asked to take her seat again.

'Mrs Denby,' the chairman of the bench said. 'I understand you are unemployed. If you have no money and no prospect of work, how are you going to support your son in the coming months and years?'

My mother defiantly remained seated. 'I don't know,' she said. 'You tell me.'

A silence resulted that was used to the prosecution's advantage. 'Wouldn't it be for the best,' said the solicitor, 'if your son was placed in care, to be looked after by professionally trained housemothers until such time as his behaviour changes for the better?'

My mother seemed not to hear his words.

'Until such time as his behaviour changes for the better, Mrs Denby.'

'Yerst, I think it would be for the best all round,' she said, unexpectedly. It was clear to everybody that her voice had suddenly become much stronger, and one or two faces turned to look at her with a quickening of interest. Equally suddenly, her bearing had become more upright. 'I think a home is the best place for him.'

The words resounded in my ears and she was looking directly at me now.

'Well,' I heard the chairman say to the solicitor, as I tried to maintain the eye contact with my mother, 'in that case sum up, Mr Agnew.'

I imagine the solicitor might have summed up like this: 'In view of the evidence we have listened to, particularly Mrs Denby's admission that her son is beyond control, and also because of the critical situation in which the child finds itself, I ask on behalf of the London County Council that a care order be made out in respect of him. It must be a question of first priority for us to see that Terence is removed from his present environment at the earliest moment for his own safety. Concern for the welfare and safety of the child are the overriding principles that have led to this action. The London County Council is willing and able to accept the responsibility of legal rights and privileges. By making an order in respect of this child you will facilitate his swift return from danger. Furthermore, Mrs Denby's conduct in leaving the boy exposed to moral danger amounts to a consistent failure on her part to discharge her obligations.'

The chairman asked me if I wished to say anything and, as I did not, which was perhaps a blessing, the magistrates retired to consider whether or not the LCC had made out its case.

It must have been a difficult mental exercise for them. It was evident that I was a little boat looking for a harbour. But how would my needs best be served? A windy home port? Or a strange, albeit calm, one? It was difficult to be optimistic in the face of such tragic alternatives. In the long term, which situation offered me the greater freedom?

When the garden gates (magistrates) returned twenty minutes later they had found the case made out and, having considered what action to take, if any, they had decided to make out an order. But the court would adjourn for three weeks to decide on the exact nature of the order and to seek a psychiatric report from a child guidance clinic. During that time I was to be kept on remand in the custody of the police. My mother and the child welfare department were given access to me.

3

Boyles Court

I don't remember anything of the actual parting from my mother. Maybe that's one thing that I have deliberately eradicated from my memory. I suppose the separation could have been messy. My mother was good at hiding her emotions, but emotionally and physically she was probably at the end of her tether. Perhaps she finally snapped. All I remember is being in the courtroom one minute and a police car the next.

Police custody meant three weeks at a remand centre for young offenders and that's where the police immediately took me.

I was confronted by a large, grim building surrounded by open fields. Inside, the classrooms, workshops and dormitories were all larger than life, and etchings of the institution's distant past proudly lined its walls, telling the usual story of development, disaster and rebuilding. There was, up to a point, still a churchy atmosphere about the place. God was mentioned in passing nearly every day. We were made to say grace before meals, taught to sing hymns, and generally trained in a manner that would be pleasing to Him.

The governor, upon whose shoulders the responsibility of discipline comfortably rested, was tall and, at the same time, very solid-looking and quite able to call from us boys the minimum amount of co-operation and respect that his job and his ego depended upon. His name was Mr Hobsbawm and he wore short, bum-freezer sports jackets with leather pads at the elbows – the kind that schoolmasters used to wear so they didn't wear out the cloth at the elbow when marking exercise books.

There were about forty other boys on remand, most of them hard nuts from the East End. I was by far the youngest to have ever crossed the threshold. Frightened by the overall strangeness of the place, I settled in as best I could.

Because of my age, six and a bit, I was looked upon by everybody as an oddity. My first afternoon passed beneath their gaze and I remember feeling hungry for the first time in my life. It was ironic. Living round The Buildings I might not have enjoyed a balanced diet, but there was always something to eat: Rolos or Liquorice Allsorts, full of the sugar that numbed any potential for an appetite. Here in the remand centre mealtimes were strictly adhered to and there was nothing in between. I had arrived after lunch and had to wait till teatime for a bite to eat.

At the appropriate hour, sausages were served up and accepted, and then I was told to wash and go to bed in my dormitory on the first landing. Mine was the Blue dormitory, where a blue light above the inside of the door burned all night. There was also the Red dormitory and the Orange, and on the second floor the Yellow, the Green, the Indigo and the Violet.

Perhaps they would keep me inside this place for ever, I thought to myself, standing on tip-toe in the washroom next morning, brushing my teeth with institutional pink powder that tasted like chalk. The other boys brushed their teeth with me over two long lines of basins, our elbows brushing vigorously, also against each other.

'Be careful,' I said, to one of the boys standing next to me. 'How much room do you need?'

'Are you talking to me or chewing a brick?' he asked, spitting into the sink, looking across and eyeballing me.

I retreated into a shell and stayed there. The driver of the police car had said there was nowhere else for me to go.

I was too young to be incarcerated with these older hooligans. And, to make things worse, I was of the opinion that I had not been torn from my mother's arms. She had let me go. And now I was subjected to a savage system. I sensed some of the staff wanted to be kind to me, but it was the system I was tied into. Everything was done at the double. It was normal to be shouted at and for tears to be met with a slap in the face. Physical violence was a way of life, every day there was a fight between boys, if not between a boy and a member of staff, kicking each other and sticking fingers in eyes. We were not allowed to keep personal possessions, so my aeroplane, which I'd managed to hold on to up to this point, was grounded. No more Pearl Harbor-ing.

There were treks through the countryside almost every day and I was carried along on them until it was realised that it wasn't fair on me or the other boys. So I was left behind with nothing better to do than walk up and down the corridors between the empty classrooms.

I hated the hymn-singing that we did in one of the smaller rooms upstairs. I disliked being packed in there like a sardine. Mr Hobsbawm would wedge himself between the baby grand and us boys; strapping youngsters some of the boys were, many of them sporting scratchy beards or sideburns which Mr Hobsbawm stressed was only bum-fluff. The piano player would strike up a tune and I would think of home. If anybody within arm's reach refused to sing, Mr Hobsbawm reached across and hit him over the head with his larger-than-life hymnbook until the boy's mouth started to move up and down. I was out of my depth, surrounded by these huge Teddy boys; as far as I was concerned, they were men. I didn't know what to do or what was expected of me, so I stood there with my mouth open and looked round from one face to another for inspiration and guidance, which was not forthcoming. I listened to the singing voices of the other boys in a kind of wonder:

> Died he for me, who caused his pain
> Died he for me, who caused his pain?

On the appointed day I was taken to see the child psychologist at the child guidance clinic in London. Mr Hobsbawm drove me there himself. It was a morning appointment on a rainy day and I sat in the back of the car and watched from the window as we proceeded through wood and common and finally emerged on to the London Road. Mr Hobsbawm then put his foot down hard on the accelerator pedal and in no time at all we were at our destination.

I was surprised to see my mother in the waiting room, sitting on a hard chair, wrapped up like a parcel in her brown coat. Nobody had bothered to tell me she was coming.

I had not seen her for two weeks and I missed her. It was a wrench being separated like this, but at the same time I blamed her for the hardships I was suffering at the remand centre. My emotions were mixed as we said hello. I sat down opposite her. I wished she had said more at the court hearing, and then I wished that she had said less. She had been so afraid of the magistrates; she had said what they wanted her to say when she might have said something helpful to me. Mr Hobsbawm said hello to my mother and then the child psychologist came and took her into the office. I recognised the psychologist; she had been to the remand centre to question other boys. She looked posh to me, dressed in a smart suit. The jacket was neatly buttoned at the front and I noticed her skirt was slim and straight and her shoes pointed.

Mr Hobsbawm and I stayed in the waiting room, and it seemed strange feeling more at home with him than my mother. I wanted her for all the reasons that children want a mother, but a wedge was being driven between us.

When my mother came out of the office she didn't even look at me. The child psychologist took me by the elbow, manoeuvred me through the doorway, and sat me down on a chair. I was not the first boy Mr Hobsbawm had brought to see her and I would not be the last. I suppose I was a classic case. A fatherless child seeking attention, and getting it. And she probably agreed with the others that what I needed more than anything was protecting from myself. I didn't say much, I found her intimidating and decided not to co-operate. Most of what she had to say went over the top of my head. As she made notes, she had a habit of repeating out loud some of the things she was writing down. She continued writing for a couple of minutes, then took a Noah's ark in kit form from under her desk and asked me to put it together. Fifteen minutes later it was still in pieces on the desk and she led me out to the waiting room, frowning and gesturing with an outstretched arm. She instructed me to say goodbye to my mother. I did, but with a kind of dissent at having to be told.

My mother uttered a synthetic farewell of her own, which aroused contempt in me. There might well have been a look of disdain on my face; for a child, two weeks is a long time in a remand centre. I nodded none the less as she mouthed 'ta ta' and, as a last bold gesture, said she would try and come to see me at the remand centre. 'What's the name of the place?' she asked.

'Boyles Court,' I replied.

'Yerst, I'll try and get down to see you.' Her face was twisted. 'As soon as I can.'

Mr Hobsbawm was talkative on the way back. He repeated to me what my mother had said to him in the waiting room about the war years, how my older half-brothers and half-sisters had been evacuated to the country. And beyond the war too, she had gone: Hobsbawm heard her stories of hop picking in Kent and Easter at Margate.

We turned off the Southend Arterial Road at Squirrels Heath and took the short cut through Jackson's Wood to the remand centre.

After lunch I joined an organised trek and was reintroduced to the country, to the smell of creosoted fences and the ivied-walls of detached houses. I did my best to keep up with the others until we passed a tramp resting against a tree and, against their better judgment, our keepers allowed us to sit down to rest on the ground beside him. Rather than pick springtime flowers, though, the older boys picked his pockets and were rewarded with some tobacco.

On Sunday I found myself again trekking through a variegated blanket of fields on my way to church. I had not been excused from going and had to be piggy-backed the last mile. As we marched, we were kept in line with sharp orders and snappy commands to do this and not to do that. Once over the common, we could see one or two houses to our left and we knew that the church and its gravestones were ahead of us on the other side of Nags Head Lane. Finally, we were outside the little village. Exhausted, I was only too glad to enter the church and kneel down on a hassock. I knelt, but I didn't believe in Jesus. As an abused child, I could not accept that Jesus was God or even good. The priest began speaking and I fell asleep.

Outside the church I joined the line of other boys, and by the time we had marched back to the remand centre for a late Sunday lunch, the sun was over the hill. Back at the centre, we washed the dishes, wiped the floors, and forgot all about God until it was time to go upstairs with Mr Hobsbawm again for hymn-singing.

When the morning arrived for me to go back to court I was told to wait in the hall until the police transport arrived. I was soon to find out what was going to happen to me.

In the grounds, boys were digging furrows in vegetable patches. Through the closed window, I could see them. And then I saw the police car at the bottom of the hill, negotiating the tight bend in the road. The boys stopped work, leaned on their shovels, and followed the car's progress with their eyes as it sped up the hill.

I knew what the boys were thinking. It wasn't difficult to read their minds. I was, after all, one of them. I couldn't have expressed it like this at the time because I was too young, but the enemy was *them* – the established system. And in a confused way we actually enjoyed our minority status and supposed inferiority. We perceived ourselves as underdogs, but at least we had status. Its quality wasn't important so long as we had some.

Mr Hobsbawm came out of his office, gave me a perfunctory look up and down, and opened the front door. 'The police car is here,' he said. 'All being well, we'll see you back here this afternoon.'

'Yes, sir,' I said mechanically.

The police car pulled up outside and I was ushered on to the back seat next to a policeman.

Mr Hobsbawm rubbed his hands together and bent down to the level of the driver's window. 'If I were you,' he said, 'I wouldn't bother with turning the car round. You can drive straight down there.' He stopped rubbing and pointed with his finger. 'Follow the track and turn right at the T-junction. It takes you past the cottage on your right and through Jackson's Wood, and then turn right again and it brings you out into Warley Road. Keep going straight ahead until you come to Squirrel's Heath and then turn right on to the London Road. Don't worry, you can't go wrong.'

The driver nodded bravely and pulled away.

I leaned back in my seat next to the uniformed officer. I felt as much at home in the police car as anywhere and I took a comb from my pocket and combed my hair as the car made its way along the track of brown earth.

The policeman looked down at me, as if knowing I would do badly in life, at school and beyond.

'How's your son? He's a happy little lad, isn't he?' The policeman in the back of the car was still looking down at me, but he was talking to the driver.

'Yes, he is. He wants a bike for his birthday.' The driver changed gear and after a pause continued: 'His mother and I will do our best to get him one.'

The policemen were talking with a kind of institutionalised indifference, as though I were not there. I decoded the signals I was getting. I could not identify with this anonymous child's happiness. All I could do was recognise my own sorrow and envy him his bike. I felt more rejected than ever, isolated, stigmatised, though I couldn't tell them that I felt this way. I could not plead my own case. How could a snotty-nosed kid plead his own case in the back of a Wolseley with a bell ringing at the front? Who could I tell? Who?

Who cared? I was confused about why I had been taken away from my mother. I felt lost, abandoned, dejected, unloved and unimportant. In my bones I knew I was unwanted and I wondered where they would finally dump me. All these experiences and negative emotions were affecting what was left of my self-worth and confidence. Some positive discrimination was needed, weighted in my favour. I was badly damaged. I had been taken away, but I felt helplessly left behind. I was being cared for by the state through no fault of my own, but through neglect and poverty.

If only I had somebody on my side, I thought to myself. But there was nobody. After three weeks at the remand centre I was even beginning to fear other children and I certainly had no trust of adults.

The police car pulled up abruptly, the way they do in films, outside the court and I was led inside by the elbow.

The magistrates, having looked at the psychiatric report from the child guidance clinic and the other relevant documents, made out a care order and let its exact nature be known. The problem, they all agreed, was more me than my mother. They found my mother fit to exercise care and guardianship over me, but unable to do so properly because I was beyond her control. And thus I was exposed to moral danger, a condition provided for under section 61 of the Children's and Young Persons' Act 1933.

I was taken in the police car back to the remand centre to wait for a suitable children's home to be found that could have me.

The following morning I was accused of something I hadn't done. Somebody had defecated on the landing outside the Blue dormitory during the night. Mr Graham, who taught us carpentry and was a tough old git, found the mess and assumed it was mine. My bed was closest to it and Mr Graham believed that it was not the action of an older boy; this was the conduct of a baby, and I was the closest thing Boyles Court had to a baby. Abusing his power, he struck me across the face as I lay in bed. He then dragged me downstairs to Mr Hobsbawm's office.

Mr Hobsbawm darkened as we went in, I on the end of Mr Graham's arm, looking like a puppet in my loose pyjamas and with the red flush crawling across my cheek where I had been hit.

The office was simply furnished with a cupboard, a few shelves and the desk that Mr Hobsbawm was sitting behind. The floor was wooden and there was an old radiator that stood out from the wall and seemed to hog the space. There was a large window facing east, and soft sunshine falling on the trees outside.

When Mr Graham explained our presence in a voice crackling with tension, Mr Hobsbawm began to look perplexed.

'Well,' was all he could think to say, as he glared at me.

I remained silent, expecting all hell to break loose again any second.

Mr Hobsbawm turned his gaze to Mr Graham. 'What do you think is wrong with the boy?'

Mr Graham, built like a bullock, hesitated for a long time with me on the end of his arm before he answered: 'Frankly, I don't know. I think it will require a psychiatrist to discover the answer to that question.'

'Have him clear it up,' Mr Hobsbawm said, with a sigh, 'and I'll punish him after breakfast.'

Many of us at Boyles Court had neurotic symptoms, and it was expected that those symptoms would manifest themselves in antisocial behaviour. We were expected to be unsure of ourselves and overcompensate with all kinds of protest. I was often punished for things I would never have thought of doing. Of course, I wasn't an angel. I had hostile feelings that sometimes became active, and I might sometimes rifle somebody's pockets because I had so often been falsely accused of doing so.

And the effects of being inadequate in the classroom and workshop bred feelings of inferiority, which in turn resulted in various escapades designed to compensate. But I did not shit on the landing.

I hardly ate any breakfast. My head was still spinning from being hit by Mr Graham. I sat at my place in the dining-hall and the thought of what Mr Hobsbawm had in mind as punishment for me after breakfast further numbed any potential for an appetite.

Eventually, tea was brought round in huge tin pots by the boys on breakfast duty. We drank, complained as was our custom that it tasted like gnats' piss, and put our hands together to say grace:

> For what we have just received,
> May the Lord make us truly thankful . . .

As I said 'Amen' I was pulled out of my chair by a tall, evil-looking senior boy named Alex Jenkins. He led me out of the dining-hall. He was a particularly vicious bully who knew how to take care of himself, and apparently he was afraid of nobody. He'd already served three years in an Approved School and was in line for Borstal for ABH after a fight in a dance hall. He took me into Mr Hobsbawm's office and closed the door.

Mr Hobsbawm was waiting, and immediately brought the cane that he had in his hand down hard on the desk. There was a vibrant crack and I knew what was in store for me. I hated my mother at that moment.

Coming towards me, he said: 'I'm going to teach you not to make a mess on the landings, or anywhere else for that matter . . .'

'It wasn't me,' I said, cowering away from his sudden advance. 'I haven't done anything.'

With a nod from Mr Hobsbawm, Alex, with a horrible smile on his face, took hold of me by the shirt and trousers and bent me awkwardly across the desk.

I heard the swish of the cane and instantaneously felt the pain. Writhing and screaming, I directed my anger towards my mother. How could she let this happen to me?

For some naïve reason, I expected Mr Hobsbawm to stop after a couple of strokes, but he didn't. He continued until it was no longer possible for me to stand it. I writhed. I screamed.

At last I was pulled away from the desk and allowed to stand up straight. Mr Hobsbawm looked down coldly at me. 'Get to your classroom and I don't want to see any more mess, anywhere, ever again. Normal children don't do that sort of thing.'

'But I didn't . . .' I cried, gripping my bottom.

'Get out of here this instant,' he roared, 'and I don't want to hear another word from you about you not being responsible for what you did.'

'But . . .' I cried, turning to Alex, looking for a mustard seed of support.

Alex's mouth tensed visibly. 'That's enough. Shut your gob.'

On Sunday I was kept away from church because of the red flush that was still visible across my face and I spent the morning walking up and down the corridors. That night I had a nightmare about nuclear war.

I was so deranged the next morning because I believed war was imminent that I was kept in bed. The other boys soon learned of what was going on and every time one of them happened to pass my dormitory they would confirm my worst fears that war had been declared and England and Russia were about to start dropping atom bombs on each other. At times I could almost taste the conflict and threatened destruction. I was contaminated with fear, convinced the whole of Essex was about to be Pearl Harbor'd, or worse, Hiroshima'd. It was horrible to contemplate. The lucky ones would be killed outright. People further away from the explosion would die slowly from overpressure the boys informed me. Whatever that was, it didn't sound nice. The wind would blow at 500 miles an hour. Burns would be third-degree and your skin would turn white – not that you would know because you would be as blind as a bat. Nuclear radiation would be in your eyes. There were other words and expressions whizzing around my bed like subatomic particles that I did not understand: groundburst, airburst, 20kt, early fallout, delayed fallout, 20M, EWP. Worst of all, I was informed there would be nobody to help you. The doctors and nurses would be dead, hospitals and fire stations flattened. There would be nowhere to go and no one to help.

I was lying in bed thinking about this when Alex Jenkins passed by on the landing.

'That's it, then. War's been declared,' he said, loud enough so that I could hear.

I noticed he had his usual ugly smile on his face as he went by. I ignored him, desperately not wanting his attention.

Two seconds later his head appeared around the edge of the door frame. He obviously didn't like being ignored. The smile had disappeared from his face and he sneered: 'The first attack will probably come tonight.'

I lay there, trying not to make eye contact, hoping he would go away and leave me alone.

But the policy backfired. He came into the dormitory, stood over my bed, put his face close to mine, and exploded: 'D'you know that one atom bomb would wipe out the whole of London and the Home Counties together?'

I felt desperate and knew I had to say something. 'D'you know what third-degree burns are, Alex?' I averted his gaze, then looked at him and looked away again.

'As it 'appens I do,' he said, moving his face even closer to mine. 'They're very deep burns. I mean *deeeep*.'

I dreamed again that night, and the more I dreamed, the more was said on the subject of nuclear war outside my dormitory. The wardens also, maliciously in my opinion, came and argued on the landing about the rights and wrongs of the use of atomic weapons against Japan in the Second World War.

It eventually became known that it wasn't my mess that Mr Graham had found on the landing. Another member of staff had reasoned with Mr Graham correctly that it wasn't the doings of a six-year-old, there had been too much.

Then, one day, another pile manifested itself on another landing and the mystery of the Phantom Crapper was established. Of course, the joke that went round was that it was probably Mr Graham.

The powers that be eventually located what they considered to be a suitable children's home for me and I was taken away from Boyles Court. But things had to get worse before they got better – much worse. In fact, you wouldn't Adam and Eve it.

4

Gibblings Shaw

The children's home was in Essex, and not a million miles from Boyles Court. The lady from the child welfare department drove me in her car, having declined the offer of a police escort. She reasoned, again correctly, that if I wanted to run away I would have ample opportunity while I was at the home and there wasn't a great deal anybody could do about it. We drew up outside in the road. Of course the house looked small compared to the remand centre, but there was a sizeable front garden and the three-storied building looked solid enough to hold me. The house name on the garden gate read 'Gibblings Shaw'.

As we approached I set eyes on the housemother for the first time. Tall with black hair, she towered over the gate. Her shoulders looked stocky and powerful beneath her buttoned-up coat and she had a scowl on her face. Above her twisted lip was the broad hint of a moustache; not just a few wisps of unwanted hair, but a dark asperity. Looking through the gaps in the gate I could see she was wearing what I now know to be a knife-pleated skirt and flat-heeled Gleneagles shoes. And she was gripping a pair of secateurs in one hand. Imagine, if you will, what I thought of that at the time as an East Ender, unaffiliated to a secateurs-wielding set! She took off her gloves and, turning away from us, without speaking stepped back to inspect her work.

A dog barked sharply, wagged its tail, and came towards us as the housemother finally acknowledged our presence and opened the gate. The dog walked towards us magnificently;

elbows free, hind legs wide, tail straight behind it, strong at the root and then tapering.

The two ladies exchanged greetings and I learned their names. Miss Abbott, the lady from the child welfare department, spoke to the dog and tickled its ears, which were hanging in neat folds close to the head, then in her own time she presented me to the housemother, Auntie Blodwen. The latter eyeballed me briefly, then turned away again.

A path ran between the flowerbeds to a buttercup-coloured front door. The door led us into a place for overcoats and umbrellas (not that I had either to deposit) and behind this vestibule another door, surrounded by a framework of stained-glass, led into a spacious hall from which ran, I soon discovered, the living-room (which they called the office), the dining-room, the children's playroom, the kitchen, the boot room and the scullery. A staircase led narrowly down to the coal-cellar in one direction and broadly up to the bedrooms in the other.

In the hall I was introduced to Auntie Agnes, the assistant housemother, and a girl about my age called Pia.

Children were already coming back from school, youngsters like myself, from broken or non-existent homes. Many of them would spend years in the care of the authority without ever knowing the warmth of family life. But all that concerned them at the moment was the arrival of me, the new boy. They brushed the evidence of school from their clothes, seemingly accepting their lot. And yet there was a woebegone look in their eyes and a suffering in the way their clothes hung from their bodies. The lethargy and sadness in their smiles, I recognised.

I was introduced straightaway to a tall curly-haired teenager. 'This is your half-brother, Tim,' Auntie Blodwen said to me. 'Do you remember each other?'

I didn't recognise him and he seemed not to know me.

'Go straight into the dining-room, both of you,' Auntie Blodwen said.

The dining-room was large, I thought. There was a dark-brown sideboard, a black, upright piano, and there were two solid tables: the Big table in the middle of the room and the Top table in the bay of the window. Both tables were laid, and what I thought was a dinner lady was passing plates of food through a service hatch. Some of the children had gathered round and were staring. I found my way to the Big table and sat down with Miss Abbott. Being an older child, Tim sat at the Top table in the bay of the window. A slightly deaf boy sat down opposite me and was introduced as George from Canning Town. When everyone was seated, the dinner lady was introduced to me as Auntie Gladys, and I was instructed by Auntie Agnes that Auntie Gladys must always be addressed as *Auntie* Gladys. And then grace was said. I'd become accustomed to saying grace before and after every meal at the remand centre.

I opened my eyes and a napkin was taken from its wooden ring and a corner of it stuffed down my jersey by the child sitting next to me. I was then introduced to the other kids and they were introduced to me.

It was for me a test of memory: Betty was George's sister, allegedly. And there was Angela; Christine, the baby, in her highchair; Henry; Constance Thweatt; Pia (she was Constance's half-sister and said that she had relatives in Drammen, just to complicate matters); Patricia; Trevor; Carole, who was Pia's sister or, if you like, Constance's half-sister; Eddy; Barry, who was Betty's and George's brother; Zsa Zsa; David; Ricky; Tony; Ena; a Janice; Jenny the dog; and a number of other animals and children. 'Come on, eat up,' Auntie Blodwen said to me in the same breath, 'we haven't all day.'

'Denby's a Welsh name, isn't it? Isn't Denby a Welsh name?' Constance asked.

I was being vigilant, expecting unpleasantness, so there was no surprise when it came.

'No it's not,' screamed Auntie Blodwen, dementedly. 'It's not spelled the same way.' She had picked up a knife and was pointing with it.

Five-year-old Constance looked down at her plate, frowned, and murmured something in Yoruba. She was as black as ebony and as hard, with tight, Afro hair. She was Pia's and Carole's half-sister, but Pia and Carole had silky blonde hair.

Emma was white as white with fair hair and was Trevor's half-sister, and Trevor was black and from India. None of this mattered to me in the least, but I sensed that Auntie Blodwen didn't like children, least of all black children in care; and, suddenly feeling angry towards her, I sat there eyeballing her.

She must have felt my eyes on her because she turned and looked at me. 'How old are you?'

'Mind your own fucking business,' I said, knowing the ground had to be tested sooner or later and it might as well be sooner.

She didn't even flinch.

There was an icy silence around the table.

Miss Abbott used the moment to finish drinking her tea and to take her leave. She shook hands with Auntie Blodwen in the doorway. 'I hope you'll be able to do something with him. You'll have to be firm.'

'Yes, I know,' said Auntie Blodwen. 'Get out of the way, Jenny.' The dog was sitting by the door, compactly. At the mention of her name she stood up on well-feathered feet. Miss Abbott patted her and then lit a cigarette. Through the dining-room window, I watched her puffing at it thoughtfully as she walked back to her car. Auntie Blodwen then took me into the office, to get acquainted.

The office was newly decorated and, to my way of thinking, looked posh. The wallpaper was masculine and striped vertically and the *look* was official, as though some kind of business were done there. A small nest of pigeon-holes for papers and messages was screwed to the wall, and yet the room still looked cosy. There were two cabinets. One of them housed the radiogram, the other was glass-fronted with ornaments and some books inside. There were two armchairs and a small settee against the wall at a straight angle to the television. On the wall above the settee was a picture of migrating geese. The carpet was wall-to-wall, a new thick-pile Wilton.

Auntie Blodwen took her time, allowed me to look around, and then she closed the door and said: 'This is for you.' She walloped me and I went flying across the room and hit a small table that stood in the bay of the window. A heavy, black telephone landed on top of me.

Her blow was so unexpected. I began to cry as rage and shock took hold of me. I bolted for the door, but she was closer. She seized me by the hair. Hauling me back, she hit me again and hurled me against the wall. Like a cartoon character, I slid down to the floor on my bottom between the television and the settee.

'Leave me alone, you fucker,' I shouted, as I tried to pick myself up.

She stood over me as I got to my knees. Her eyes were distended and she had an ugly set to her mouth.

'Get out of my way,' I said, sweeping a forearm towards her to brush her aside. She flung an arm up and deflected my move. Even so, I managed to hit her in the side with my other fist and the sudden discomfort made her eyes bulge out of their sockets.

Hitting her was a mistake because all hell broke loose. Her face livid, she rained blows down on me one after the other and finally kicked me to the floor in a heap.

'Let that be a warning to you,' she hissed, opening the door. The short but heated baptism was over.

I was content to escape with my life and, picking myself up, retreated into the hall. The other children were lined up and being reined in by Auntie Agnes, real fear showing on their faces. There was little chance of Tim or any of them coming to my rescue.

'Would you like to give Terry a bath?' Auntie Blodwen said to Auntie Agnes. 'He smells.' She could not disguise the agitation in her voice.

Auntie Agnes took me by the ear and I experienced a massive, inescapable defencelessness. I was led upstairs to a bathroom. Stripping off my clothes, Auntie Agnes sat me in a bath of hot water.

I was now totally exposed to the wilfulness and madness of these adults, a madness that readily coexisted with a polished sociability so that it remained invisible to the outsider. The housemothers were invested with important positions and enjoyed respect in the community. But behind closed doors they were taking out the repressed torture of their own childhoods on the children in their care. They were regarded as being excellent housemothers by the powers that be at the 'home office' (that is, the office at the LCC child welfare department, not the government department responsible for law and order and immigration in England and Wales and run by the Home Secretary), but were blind to the needs of the children in their care because they both learned as young girls that a child's needs count for nothing. They never received the necessary care and orientation from their own mothers and did not like to be reminded of that fact by having to empathise with unhappy children – even though Auntie Agnes was once that same child, having spent time in care herself as a youngster.

I was becoming more self-conscious by the second. 'Can't I get out now?' I asked.

'You can get out when you have washed yourself. Wash your feet. *Wash* them. Don't you enjoy bath time?' Auntie Agnes handed the soap to me.

I shrugged my small shoulders as the large square of soap slipped unmanageably from my hand and into the water. Auntie Agnes fished around for it as she ordered me to stand up.

Then she was called away and Patricia was told to finish me off.

I was indignant. I didn't appreciate Patricia seeing me without my clothes on. In fact, Patricia and I both felt uncomfortable with the arrangement. She was ten years old, there was no familial tie between us, and she seemed interested in my nakedness.

I was put to bed early in a dormitory on the first landing, furnished with five metal-framed beds and a solitary chest of draws. I'd had a long day, what with one thing and another, from the remand centre to the home, to a good hiding. Before falling into an uncomfortable sleep I listened to bees droning through the open window and watched birds circling on a summery wind. Auntie Blodwen and Auntie Agnes, I learned surprisingly quickly, were not interested in the birds and the bees.

My nightmare began with the sound of an aeroplane approaching. Engines droning, it came through the clouds and into view. It was a bomber. The drone of the engines was continuous, the same monotonous sound, and the aeroplane was surrounded by a sort of strange atmosphere that is not easy to explain away. The bomb-doors opened and in slow motion a bomb came out of the belly of the aeroplane and fell towards the ground. Then it was quiet. Except for ZZZZZZZZ, as if something more wicked than the bomb was free at last; ZZZZZZZZs inside was its outside and its back was its front. It was heavy, but faceless and empty. I couldn't iron it out. Then I realised it was me. I was the bomb. I clawed at thin air to get back inside the aeroplane, but it was too late.

The explosion killed and destroyed indiscriminately. West Ham Underground station and The Buildings collapsed into heaps of rubble and the power station's two giant cooling towers bowed out gracefully with that core of dignity perceptible in all monolithic artefacts as they fall to dust. Railway lines melted, gasometers exploded, trolleybuses and trains went up in white smoke, and a big wave flooded the Royal Victoria Dock. Then a sudden hot wind blew and battered the debris into mounds which were driven across the ground in galaxies of chaos. The air was full of flying objects. I dreamed I saw the furniture from the flat being blown along by the wind, broken and smashed. The three-piece suite and straight-backed chairs tumbled over and over until they were indistinguishable from the general disorder. And then the aeroplane was caught by the wind and I watched as it was blown along sideways and finally crashed into the ground and became part of the whirlwind in a deafening explosion and blinding blue flash.

I opened my eyes and at the same moment I became convinced there was a bomb in the room. I closed my eyes again and sweat ran down my chest until my pyjamas and the bedclothes were soaked and I was afraid of the dark; and when I could stand it no longer, I screamed at the top of my voice.

I lay in bed screaming like Lord Sutch and remembered what had been said at the remand centre: 'Tactical nuclear bombs do not have the horrible side-effects of strategic ones'. And then a second voice making nonsense of the first: 'All nuclear bombs kill civilians and ruin the countryside'. In my nightmares I was responsible for a strategic nuclear war. I began to feel weighed down with guilt.

Auntie Blodwen rushed into the dormitory in her nightdress and switched on the light, not knowing what to expect. The house could be on fire and the animals choking. She found everything in order except me. For a second, she seemed lightheaded with relief. Then she cursed me loudly, but her voice was drowned by my own shrill cries that would not abate. Little by little, her shouting got the better of me and I eventually stopped screaming. The other boys in the room were sitting bolt upright in their beds.

It was nearly dawn and clouds were tangled over the sky. I lay there and only my eyes moved, quickly darting from Auntie Blodwen to the other boys, to the window and back to Auntie Blodwen. She reached down and, gripping the bedclothes with both hands, pulled the counterpane, the blanket and the sheet from the bed in one swift movement. Everything grew suddenly very still and the room became cold. A few last words came out of her mouth like the dribblings of a dragon as she looked down at my body hidden inside wet pyjamas. She stared, and her anger, which a second earlier had been enough to kill me, turned to a look of utter disgust and I stared back wide-eyed. I wanted to cover myself, but resisted as she began to beat me around the head and neck in a flash of cold fury, regarding me through narrowed eyes as my taut body shrank into the mattress. I began to sob. She took no notice, and her look of disgust now turned to a mocking smile.

* * *

In the middle bathroom it was quiet and cool as I looked out of the open window above the sink and nursed my wounds. I could see the tops of two trees that were close to the house, and the branches of another at the far end of the garden. I would have stayed longer, observing my new habitat, if Trevor hadn't come into the bathroom looking for me. He had straight, jet-black hair and coffee-coloured skin and he was wearing his school uniform. Chivvying me on, he spoke hurriedly. 'Get into your uniform and downstairs quickly, you're late.' Trevor was being cruel to be kind. He too knew the wrath of Auntie Blodwen.

I returned to the bedroom and put on a school uniform that had been thrown down for me on the end of the bed.

In the following days and weeks I learned more about my new surroundings. The number of children at the home varied; there was a certain amount of coming and going. Some stayed for days, others for years. I don't remember seeing much of my half-brother, Tim. He was a lot older than me and had his own friends. And anyway, he left quite soon after I arrived. We spent Christmas together and then I don't remember him being around any more. One day he was there, the next he was gone. At fifteen he was old enough to get a job, earn his keep and pay his way; under those circumstances, I suppose my mother was prepared to have him back!

Usually there were about eighteen or nineteen of us at the children's home. Auntie Gladys, the cook, came in during the week and there were two cleaners who came during the morning. There was also a tall, slim gardener-cum-handyman who wore loose clothing and a tight belt and he seemed to simply pop in from time to time. And last, but by no means least, there were the animals: the dog, which I now knew to be an Irish setter; two cats, a ginger one and a grey one; and a very large black rabbit.

A dentist lived and worked next door. He thought the home was a little too close for comfort and was forever threatening us over the fence. 'Keep your voice down, can't you?' he shouted across to Trevor one evening. Trevor was simply calling out to me at the other end of the back garden. I was close to the fence. 'Bloomin' wogs,' I heard the dentist say.

On another occasion there were several groups of us playing in the back garden and somebody accidentally knocked a ball over the fence. The dentist quickly approached his side of the fence, gesticulating with the ball in his hand. We stopped playing immediately. 'I've told you once too often,' he barked, 'not to allow the ball to come into my garden . . .'

'Can we have it back?' Constance asked. She was wearing clothes that were several sizes too big for her, but she couldn't help looking pretty.

'No, you may not,' he said. 'And stop all that yelling. For crying out loud, it sounds like feeding time at a zoo. I don't know what the country's coming to.'

'We couldn't help it,' Constance replied, bravely.

'No, you never can help it, can you? Nigger.'

As a young boy growing up in care, I learned the difference between a 'nigger' and a 'wog' and I learned also that you didn't have to be uneducated to be racist; you just had to be not very intelligent.

I learned nothing about the elderly couple who lived on the other side, but either way the immediate neighbours would have nothing to do with the home. They believed the stigma affected the value of their property, and they had their doubts about Auntie Blodwen and Auntie Agnes too. A home like that should be run by a *proper* couple, a man and a woman. Even at the tender age of six I could read their 1950s minds.

My bedroom was above the playroom, I discovered, and all three bathrooms were conveniently off my landing, a matter of going down four wooden steps as I turned right out of the bedroom.

I soon learned just how stern and unpredictable Auntie Blodwen could be. She was omnipresent, omniscient and omnipotent, not to say ominous and an avid reader of the Bible. She also read the Book to us, thus demonstrating and confirming to herself that her method of childrearing was perfectly right. When she had a mind to, she would take us into the office, make herself comfortable in an armchair, and sit us down on the floor in front of her. As she read from the Authorised Version we struggled to get to grips with Noah's ark and rainbows, Joseph and his coat of many colours, and hard times in Egypt. I remember particularly the time she read us the story of the baby Moses:

> And there went a man of the house of Levi,
> And took to wife a daughter of Levi.
> And the woman conceived, and bare a son:
> And when she saw him that he was a goodly child,
> She hid him three months.
> And when she could not longer hide him,
> She took for him an ark of bulrushes,
> And daubed it with slime . . .
> [Exodus 2:1–3]

'Was the ark the same as Noah's ark?' I asked.

'No, you idiot,' she said, without taking her eyes off the

page. 'It was a little basket. And talking of little baskets, don't interrupt until I've finished.'

She sought comfort in the Bible, it gave her hope. The reality for us children was different. We were led to believe that the cruelty we were enduring was because of our own wickedness. Our only hope was that one day we could stop being bad. It was just punishment. After all, one can stop being bad. We burdened ourselves with more and more guilt. I found it especially wicked having a choice of bathrooms, with running hot water in each, even that seemed greedy. And greed was sinful. Although we resented having it forced down our throats and hated going to church, religion rubbed off on us. For children in a children's home, the idea of having a father in heaven was appealing, even if we were not good enough to be acceptable to him. And so as children we started to discuss God, perhaps up at the dining-room table or in the playroom, as though his existence were a real possibility. Some of us started to believe. Before going to sleep, I for one said my prayers – even though Auntie Blodwen had no way of knowing if I had said them or not. This was one of the few things I had control over. I recited the same prayers every night, a little out of fear, a little out of longing.

When I went to sleep Auntie Blodwen was in my dreams. I would wake up at night in the dark and want to cry out, but there was nobody who would listen sympathetically. I would get out of bed and stand at the top of the stairs, afraid to go down towards the beckoning light that shone from under the office door, but afraid also to go back to my bed. I survived another night and day. I learned very quickly not to turn to others when I was afraid, but to cope on my own.

Auntie Blodwen's father had a room at the home, the sick-room, which should have been used to isolate us children when we were not well. It was against the rules, but the LCC knew nothing about the arrangement. He was short and plump and divested of most of his hair. A music critic-cum-journalist, he was away on business most of the time. But he made good use of the home's facilities when he was around. He was from somewhere near Merthyr Tydfil, I think, and that's where Auntie Blodwen was from originally, I suppose.

When Pop was away on business (we called him Pop because he was a sort of grandfather figure) we would be isolated in the sick-room if we were contagiously ill, but Pop's things would still be in the cupboard, his uniform hung in the wardrobe with all its trimmings, and his typewriter on the table.

I saw him for the first time through the service hatch when I was having a day off school with a cold. He was in the dining-room and a bit like a little hobbit, although not half as shy; he was enjoying a second little breakfast, thinking perhaps that another slice of toast or two and another drink of tea would do him good. Auntie Gladys was serving him through the hatch and he was reading the newspaper as he ate. 'The United States of America is preparing to explode another hydrogen bomb,' I heard him say. That was all I needed to hear.

Draining his cup of tea, he got up from the table, went over to the piano, and began to play. I was more than used to hearing a piano. A piano was for listening to. So I went into the dining-room and received some of the blessings that a piano can bring, although I must say the music was strange to my ears. Pop hardly acknowledged my presence and I discovered in due course that he deliberately kept a distance between himself and all the children at the home. We didn't take it to heart at the time, but looking back I think it was snobbery, pure and simple. It wouldn't have been the done thing at the time for him to mix with the likes of us, not in that neck of the woods. He never went to church, though, and that endeared us to him up to a point. (I learned in due course that Pop had returned from the Second World War disillusioned with religion: going to war a convicted Protestant, coming back an atheist, and having as little to do with the Church as possible from then on.)

Auntie Gladys came through with the post and placed it on the Big table. 'That's nice music,' she said, and off she went with a frown, leaving me wondering if she really did think it was nice.

Pop stopped playing and began to open his letters as a cat, the grey one, came scrounging round the table looking for a titbit, mewing loudly. It was Auntie Blodwen's cat, an ordinary domestic tabby.

The weeks and months passed and one Sunday morning a new homeless yoblet arrived. He came with Miss Abbott. Through the closed dining-room window I saw her drive up, business-like, and pace round to the car's nearside door to escort the seven-year-old into the house.

The boy came through the door and looked at each of us in turn. We gazed back at him. He had brown hair, which was darker in some places than others. It was cut in a fringe across the forehead and was short at the sides so that his ears, which were large and red, stuck out. He was wearing a black jersey with yellow stripes on the sleeves, short grey trousers, and heavy-duty beetle-crushers on the end of remarkably short legs. He looked like a salamander with boots on.

I was no longer the new boy and I gratefully led him up the hill to church.

5

Church

Handbag firmly tucked under her arm, Auntie Blodwen knelt down next to me, looking for trouble.

It was a flint and limestone building with stained-glass windows and a pigeon-infested ramparted tower with a flag on top. Inside, two wide aisles led up to the altar between the rows of hardwood pews on which the congregation sat formally facing the front. To the right of the altar was an arched recess that housed the organ, and the pulpit was elevated next to the choir-stalls opposite. Shafts of sunlight pierced the stained-glass windows and fell across us 'cared-for' children. We filled three pews. I sat there trying to make sense of the grovelling figure kneeling next to me. She looked like a praying mantis. The priest began to speak, and this genuflecting stick insect beside me sat back in the pew while, as a distraction, I fixed my eyes on a tapestry depicting the Spirit's descent.

I can't really remember – it was too long ago and he spoke too quickly – but in keeping with the times I suppose there would have been a proper ethic of *service* in the words that Father Worthington spoke to us on that Sunday morning: an ethic of social improvement and social aspiration, linked to some view of Jesus Christ as a paragon of the virtuous citizen. I have a vague recollection of a reference to Billy Graham, the American evangelist. He was on his first crusade in Britain at the time, and although I can't remember precisely what Father Worthington said about him, his few words were kind and welcoming. Billy Graham believed that anyone could be saved, and his charismatic style was unlike anything that had been seen in English churches for a long time. But he was a fellow Protestant, so that was all right.

A collect was uttered and we kids were sent off to Sunday school. We filed out of church into the hall at the back, aware that Auntie Blodwen was watching us. This was 1954; children still attended Sunday school where the supplementary religious education went on, a vital, added dimension to the week, with denominational flavouring. And as we were not ready to take on board abstract ideas, Sunday school had to be child-centred, the teaching based on our capacity to learn, not didactically, but inductively. We would start with a theme – perhaps 'Holidays' – and then explore that theme from as many angles as possible, including religious and spiritual, putting the emphasis on our own interests and on our own discovery. So religion was about life, and about life as it affects everyone, not just religious people. Sunday school was no longer supposed to provide the answer to life, it was a building block. We weren't given the recipe, but we were given the ingredients. That was the developmental theory.

At our Sunday school a man in a suit usually read a story from the Old Testament relevant to the morning's theme, which line by line decayed into the old patter: the promise of reward and redemption for obedience, punishment for disobedience, and outbursts of violence and obsessional destructiveness from the Loving Creator.

I used to sit and fidget while he decried my sins. I wasn't interested in reward or redemption, whatever that meant. The suited gentleman's days were numbered and it wasn't long before I challenged his authority.

We were seated in the hall at the back of the church and he was standing in front of us telling a story about a donkey that could talk. I admit to being dim but I wasn't *that* stupid. I turned to the boy next to me and started to giggle. The Sunday school teacher ignored me and continued with the story until it got to the point where I felt I had to say something.

'Donkeys can't talk,' I shouted from the back row.

He lowered his Bible, took a deep breath, and looked up. 'That's the whole point,' he said. 'They can if God tells them to.'

'But if God wanted donkeys to talk, why didn't he make them that way?' I was rewarded with a short laugh for this line from the other children, my audience.

'Don't you get it?' the Sunday school teacher hit back. 'Even an ass could understand.' He looked down at the pages of his Book and then looked up again. 'You're from Gibblings Shaw, aren't you?'

I made a noise like a donkey and earned the louder laugh I wanted.

'I should have known,' he said.

When I returned to Gibblings Shaw I was in trouble with Auntie Blodwen, of course. Waiting for me in the hall as I arrived, she approached and towered over me with a menacing expression on her face. I felt so small. I was nothing big; just a kid, and gazing up at her helplessly I wondered why she even bothered to notice me. But notice me she did.

'I don't know what in the name of God I'm going to do with you,' she screeched in my ear, leaning down and putting her head close to mine. Her breath was hot on my face and smelled like mothballs. She remained there, motionless, waiting for a response from me. There was none.

My insides turned over with fear and apprehension as, grabbing hold of me by the hair, she suddenly flung me into the office through the open door. She slammed the door closed behind her, her voice becoming icier. 'Don't you think this place has a bad enough reputation as it is without you adding insult to injury by going to Sunday school and calling the teacher an ass?'

This lop-sided account of what was said actually un-fuddled my brain up to a point and I protested: 'I didn't call him an ass.'

'Stop telling lies,' she screamed, walloping me across the face with the back of her hand and causing me to reel backwards. 'On top of everything, you have the audacity to stand there and protest your innocence.' Grabbing hold of my hair again, she led me across the room and banged my head against the partition wall.

'I'll knock some sense into that thick head of yours,' she yelled.

Fear made my breathing difficult and, in spite of the hammering, my head felt light through lack of oxygen. The wall shook with each impact and I thought my head would break. I knew that the children in the playroom next door were suffering quietly, too. I'd often been in the playroom myself when other children were beaten up in the office. I wasn't the only one. The shouting and screaming easily penetrated the thin wall and I would pace up and down the playroom wondering whose turn it was going to be next. The other children at the home were like brothers and sisters to me and, listening to their screams, especially if it was one of the girls, was enough sometimes to make me want to run into the office and take their place.

Auntie Blodwen banged my head against the wall one more time and my legs finally gave way beneath me. From somewhere I found the breath to breathe an obscenity:

'You fucker.'

She ignored my language and hauled me out into the hall. She then flung me through the open door of the playroom on to the floor in front of the other kids, a massive humiliation.

I have to own up to being drawn back to the church hall in

due course by the need for community. I needed friends and I became a Cub Scout. My fingernails were inspected by Akela; she tut-tutted, shook her head in dismay, and admitted me.

The next time I went to Sunday school I was in my Cub Scout uniform; green beret with the Cub motif pinned to it, green jersey, a neckerchief edged with the colours of the Pack: the man in the suit must have thought he was winning the battle for my soul. He got down to business straight away and said that owning a television was like having a sewer running through your front room.

I remember sitting there thinking that this didn't stop the priest from coming to the children's home to watch the University Boat Race on our 12-inch Ferg. The rat. He used to bring his wife and four children along and they supported Cambridge. There was a relaxation during these visits of the formality that we were used to in church, and once when the Irish setter rubbed her rear end against Auntie Blodwen's leg and Auntie Blodwen said 'No sex today, thank you', neither the priest nor any member of his family batted an eyelid, but cheered Cambridge on all the louder.

Auntie Blodwen physically and mentally lambasted me for wetting the bed. She noticed the smell and the dampness the minute she pulled the bedclothes off me when she came into the dormitory. Not wanting to touch me, she took a book from a bedside table and began to beat me with it around the body, my wet skin making the whacks especially painful. She then prodded me out of bed with the book. 'You filthy little guttersnipe,' she screamed in my ear. She was obviously furious at the thought of having to deal with the soiled sheets. She slapped and pushed me with the book out on to the landing where I stood shivering.

'Don't just stand there,' she shouted. 'Go to the bathroom and wash yourself.'

I did as I was told as quickly as possible. In the bathroom I took my wet pyjamas off and threw them into the laundry basket. Cold and naked, I stood in front of the sink and washed.

During breakfast I was presented with a watering-can. It was ironic, but a watering-can was what I had asked for as a present for my seventh birthday. I had never lived in a house with a garden, but flowers and plants intrigued me and, with the arrival of spring, I decided to make them grow bigger and smell stronger. I decided I would make the tree at the bottom of the garden grow taller; it was too easy-peasy to climb this tree and I needed more of a challenge. But it was a small, red watering-can and I was disappointed, because it was more like a toy than the real thing. If this weren't enough to spoil a birthday, during breakfast we were told that we were going to church that evening, so not to be late back from school. It was St George's Day and the vicar was expecting us to attend the special St George's Day Service.

At school during the afternoon we were given flags and taken by our teachers to the main road to join hundreds of others as the Queen Mother passed by in a black Rolls-Royce on her way to Trooping the Colour by the First Battalion, the Manchester Regiment, at Brentwood.

We returned to the home in a military frame of mind, marching from the top of the hill like the Grand Old Duke of York's Ten Thousand, equally respectable in our school uniforms. After tea I changed into my Cub Scout's uniform. I was marched up the hill again. Front doors along the road opened and closed, closely followed by the garden gate, until soon there was a saintly procession heading in one direction.

On arrival at the church I joined my group of Cub Scouts, 28th Epping Forest, and we paraded in front of the choir-stalls as the choir members, in black robes and white surplices, emerged from the vestry and took their places. I lifted my flag high; the red and white cross of St George of England. Father Worthington walked past, admiring my flag, his square chin and his perfectly straight teeth complemented by a broad smile. I felt important for once, and although I was put wise to the constitution of flags at an early age, I've grown up to view them as divisive.

We then knelt down and the priest absolved us of our sins: 'Almighty God the Father of our Lord Jesus Christ, who desireth not the death of a sinner, but rather that he may turn from his wickedness and live; and hath given power and commandment to his Ministers, to declare and pronounce to his people, being penitent, the Absolution and Remission of their sins: He pardoneth and absolveth all them that truly repent and unfeignedly believe his holy Gospel. Wherefore let us beseech him to grant us true repentance and his Holy Spirit, that those things may please him which we do at this present, and that the rest of our life hereafter may be pure and holy; so that at the last we may come to his eternal joy . . .'

I leaned towards the Cub Scout to my left and whispered that I liked Bill Haley's version of 'Rock Around the Clock'.

He answered: 'Amen.'

The priest said: 'O Lord. Open thou our lips.'

And I sang: 'When the clock strikes five, six and seven, we'll be rockin' up in seventh heaven . . .'

I hadn't realized how far my voice would carry, reverberating off those flint and limestone walls and echoing under the church's hammerbeam roof. The priest looked up, surprised, and said: 'O God, make speed to save us.'

I looked down, but I knew that Auntie Blodwen was looking across at me and that I had gone too far this time.

The Psalm was followed by the first lesson taken out of the

Old Testament, not as appointed in the Church Calendar, but a special lesson assigned for that day. The reader read with a distinct voice, standing and turning himself so that he could be heard by all. In like manner the second lesson was read out of the New Testament, a hymn was sung, and the Apostles' Creed was said.

Three more collects were uttered before Father Worthington climbed the steps into the pulpit and delivered his prepared sermon. 'Imagine, if you will,' he began, 'St George making that journey to the Holy Land. Or imagine somebody making a modern-day journey in a motor car. It's raining, it's dark . . .'

And then he went on about illuminated signs and arrows and how it never crosses the motorist's mind that they could be pointing the wrong way. 'We trust the signposts,' he said. 'We have faith in them.'

The Anthem was sung, closely followed by prayers. I remember that the prayer leader, whether it be Father Worthington or a member of the congregation, was always selective about who we prayed for. The prayers were always for teachers, for Her Majesty the Queen or for social workers, doctors and nurses. Teachers were prayed for the most. But I never once heard a prayer for a lorry driver, or a labourer, or for a stevedore, a boiler cleaner, a steel-erector's mate, a bus driver or a painter and decorator. The prayers were anything but common. As the prayers were concluded, the Scouts were the vanguard, the first to march out of the church carrying their large, heraldic flags before them. The Cub Scouts followed behind.

As always, Father Worthington shook hands at the porch with as many people as possible and a queue formed as one parishioner stopped for an inordinate length of time to talk. I'd put my flag away and was making my way outside through the crush.

'I enjoyed your sermon, anyway,' I heard the parishioner say, 'even if it was a bit Catholic.'

I wondered what he meant.

Father Worthington turned and glad-handed the next person in the queue.

Outside in the graveyard, as dusk fell, there was a general gathering. Auntie Blodwen sought out Akela, the Cub Scout leader. They chatted for a moment and then Akela adjusted her toggle, gave the two-fingered salute, and escaped.

We were marched down the hill again to Gibblings Shaw.

'Wait here,' Auntie Blodwen said to me, as we entered the house. She went into the office with Auntie Agnes and left me standing in the hall. The other children went into the cloakroom and took their coats off.

As I waited I became more and more tense, knowing I was probably in line for a good hiding. After what seemed like an age, the office door opened and Auntie Blodwen's voice exploded in my face: 'Get yourself in here.' She grabbed me by the sleeve of my coat and pulled me aggressively into the room. Her voice still sharp-tempered, she asked me what was the meaning of singing in church at the top of my voice when Father Worthington was trying to conduct a service.

'I didn't mean it,' I said feebly.

'No,' she said, 'you never mean anything, do you?' She turned away from me and went over to the glass-fronted cabinet and picked up a wooden ruler that had been placed on the top of it. The two women exchanged glances and then Auntie Agnes grabbed hold of me and undid the belt and buttons of my short trousers, allowing them to fall around my ankles. She then pulled down my underpants and bent me forwards. My Cub Scout's cap fell off my head on to the floor. Auntie Blodwen was now standing behind me, and grabbing hold of the back of my coat she began hitting me with the ruler. It didn't hurt much because the ruler was so short she couldn't build up any impetus in her strokes, but the humiliation was massive. I struggled and so did they, trying to hold me still in a position where Auntie Blodwen could build up some momentum as she brought the ruler down on me. They couldn't get it right. In the end it became a joke. And that was the most crushing thing, the joke was on me. I fixed my gaze on my cap and waited for them to stop it.

In the autumn of that year the suited gentleman at Sunday school instructed us to learn by heart Psalm 121 from the Authorised Version of the Bible. A week later I surprised everyone, including myself, by being the first to do so:

> I will lift up mine eyes unto the hills,
> from whence cometh my help.
> My help cometh from the Lord . . .

I recited at the front of the class, and instead of saying 'cometh' I said 'comet', because I thought the psalm was talking about help coming in a jet aeroplane. The man in the suit must have thought I had a speech defect.

My mind was not really on the Lord, but aeroplanes and Guy Fawkes. In a few days I would lift up mine eyes to the sky from whence cometh fireworks. Even here, though, there were religious connotations. We'd been told at school that Guy Fawkes was a Counter-Reformationist and an enemy of the Protestant James I. We, nevertheless, were looking forward to Guy Fawkes's night. By seven o'clock on 5 November the bonfire was well-ablaze between the sycamore and the silver birch and lit up the garden with a yellow glow and warmed the festive faces of everyone standing around. I stood mesmerised. Crackers jumped in the dentist's garden next door, and on the other side Vesuvius volcanoes erupted in front of the two elderly ladies who lived at number 33. Meanwhile, at the end of my outstretched arm, a Roman candle glowed dangerously, albeit less sinisterly than the votive candles in church. Unsuggestive of evil, this one glowed right. As expected, it burst into brilliant flame. No surprises with these, you knew exactly what you were getting for your money. A badly aimed rocket from the dentist's base zoomed overhead out of control. Maybe the dentist was trying to get us, I thought, following its flight path. But, after a moment of suspense, the missile harmlessly banished its flickering payload to the void before falling silently back to earth. Auntie Blodwen irresponsibly let off a penny banger close behind me as I was on this flight of fancy with my mouth open, and the loud bang ended my memory of Guy. I came back to the twentieth century with a start. Perhaps she's human after all, I thought.

Following her bad example, I took a jumping cracker from my pocket, lit the end, and threw it down on the grass in front of her.

'You fool,' she screamed, turning and running.

The cracker started jumping and I earnestly hoped it would jump in her direction. But instead it went zigzagging towards the boiler-room where the fireworks were stored. Sure enough, the boiler-room door was open and the cracker jumped right inside. It was suddenly no longer funny. Father Worthington was present with his family and, leaving their side, he dashed into the boiler-room and managed to kick the firework outside again with his foot. Everybody retreated and the cracker exhausted itself on the terrace. Father Worthington went back into the boiler-room to check that the store of fireworks was intact. When he reappeared everyone applauded, except Auntie Blodwen, of course. By the look she gave me I think she could have killed me. If the priest and his family hadn't been there, I think she would have thrown me on the bonfire.

I got to know the Reverend and Mrs Worthington and they took me under their Anglo-Catholic wing, in the knowledge that this was one of the ends for which they had been created, to visit the fatherless in their affliction. Their home was very comfortable. The dining-room table was solid and the cutlery polished. There was fine lace and cut-glass in the cupboards which came out at regular intervals. I thought I could probably get used to it. But this was a passing acquaintance with family life, nothing more. How naïve of me to think otherwise. Father Worthington's calling was only to visit the fatherless, not to love them as his own.

It wasn't my family, but I spent more and more time at the priest's house, sometimes overnight, sharing my nightmares and meals with them and their four children. Mrs Worthington cooked cauliflower cheese, which she knew I liked, and if I'd known how to, I might have loved her. She was there for me, far from the female father-figures of Gibblings Shaw.

Our local MP, Sir Winston Churchill, resigned as prime minister and was succeeded by Sir Anthony Eden. And then round about the same time, having been encouraged by the success of his first visit to Britain, Billy Graham returned and targeted Scotland. Father and Mrs Worthington never took me to see him, thank God, but instead made plans to take me camping in the summer on the edge of the forest. I thought I could never be equal to them, what with my nightmares and bedwetting, but in the event my social acceptability took a turn for the better as I slept longer and dreamed less. I was, after all, on holiday and eight years old now.

6

Primary School

There were two sides to me, an inside and an outside. The outside could be recognised as a Cub Scout, a boy playing football, letting off fireworks, going to church, learning a psalm, camping, eating and sleeping. Simply looking at me, a complete stranger might have thought I was normal. I had the resilience that all children have, whatever their circumstances. It would take more than continually being beaten, insulted and ridiculed, not to mention the loss of my family, to stop me playing and generally amusing myself with the distractions of an eight-year-old.

The pain was hidden and you had to get to know me to see it. If grown-ups looked carefully, my smile was unhappy and my laugh empty, the laugh of an orphan which, if listened to carefully, sounds hollow.

So with the start of the new school year, I was reminded that I had moments of personal crisis to deal with. Sometimes at school, along with the other cared-for children, I was called a 'dirty orphan' and excluded from some activity or other.

It was a mixed school, but there was sexual segregation; there were girls' classrooms and boys' classrooms and the only place the boys met the girls was in the playground. I remember in the playground once trying to defend a girl from Gibblings Shaw who was being ridiculed by some of the other boys. Angela was always wetting herself, and to punish her Auntie Blodwen would send her to school without any knickers.

She was playing hop, skip and jump on this particular morning, and when her state of undress became apparent, the boys were falling over themselves laughing and trying to lift up her dress.

'Leave her alone, you fuckers,' I shouted, going towards the group of boys. Angela was older than me, but I felt strangely protective towards her, as if she were my sister.

A boy called Jack Philips emerged from the group of boys and came towards me. 'What's that, Denby?' He was the up-and-coming son of a local chartered accountant. Philips was tall for his age, with a substantial frame, and he boasted of being the best fighter in the class.

'Leave her alone,' I repeated. 'She hasn't done anything.'

'But she doesn't have any knickers,' he laughed. 'Fancy, girls coming to school without knickers. Can't they afford them at Gibblings Shaw . . .?' With this, the other boys started to laugh too.

He was standing in front of me now and waiting to see what I would do. The laughter died away.

'It's not her fault,' I said.

'My father said I should keep away from you orphans.'

'Why don't you, then?' I replied.

'And why don't you get back to where you belong? Dirty orphan.' With this, he put his left foot behind my right ankle and pushed me backwards, causing me to go sprawling on my back and hitting my head on the hard ground. At the same moment, the bell went.

It was hard to stand up, and by the time I had got to my feet and brushed myself down, the other children had disappeared from the playground. I stood still for a second in the sudden quietness, orienting myself. My head throbbed and I knew instinctively that my arm was grazed beneath my blazer. Realising I was going to be late, I then dashed into the school building after the others.

The headmaster, Mr Carr, was in the corridor and he stopped me immediately with an outstretched arm. He was a large man, and running into him was like hitting a barricade. 'How many times must you be told not to run in the corridors?' he shouted. He was obviously vexed.

'I'm late sir,' I said feebly, looking anywhere except up at him.

'But why are you late? Is it so difficult to go to your classroom when you hear the bell go?'

'No, sir.'

He thought for a moment. 'You're from Gibblings Shaw, aren't you?'

'Yes, sir.'

He sighed. 'I might have known. Get to your classroom. And straighten your tie before you go in. You look like a village lout.'

When I went into the classroom Mr Thomas stood up behind his desk, surprised. He hadn't, apparently, noticed my absence. The other boys had their heads down and were writing, except for Philips who was looking across at me with an expression of delight on his face.

'Why are you late?' Mr Thomas asked, sternly.

'The Headmaster wanted to talk to me,' I replied.

This answer seemed to pacify him up to a point, and he ordered me to go to my desk and sit down. 'Copy what's on the blackboard into your exercise book,' he said.

I took out my book and dipped the nib of my pen into the sunken reservoir of ink. I began to scribble, nervously.

I was the last to finish and everybody was watching and waiting. It was not my vocation to write. I was way off-task and I sat there waiting to be mocked and laughed at.

'Well, come on, Denby,' Mr Thomas said, standing up. 'We haven't all day.'

He strode over to my desk and looked down at my exercise book. He tut-tutted and rolled his eyes around the classroom.

This was the signal for the other boys to break out into uproarious laughter, and as they did so, I lowered my head in shame. At school and beyond, everybody without exception treated me like an underdog. No wonder I worked and behaved like one.

My sense of loss at losing my parents did diminish, but only in the sense that I was anaesthetised by other people's spite, and drunk with victimisation. What I mean is, how could I go on feeling? At the back of my mind I always knew I was different, but I was not ready to fight back, not quite.

I would soon learn, though, and my retaliation would manifest itself in more bad work and even worse behaviour, but also in trying to be funny. Feeling friendless one day in the playground, I approached a group of boys:

'Do you know why the lady standing outside her front door with a £5 note in each ear was crying?' I asked.

'Go on,' one of them said.

'Because her rent was in arrears.'

That was my entrance liturgy and I very soon cottoned on to the fact that I could make them laugh not *at* me, but *with* me. I began to do it without thinking. I now had a line of control and this gave me the confidence to start behaving really badly, at school and elsewhere.

Pupils went to the school from a wide area including some *pur sang* villages as far afield as Epping. Every year the school was heavily over-subscribed. The school claimed, of course, that this was due to its own distinctive atmosphere.

During the time I spent there, the buildings were restructured and modernised and complemented by the Assembly Hall that backed on to the forest. In the new Assembly Hall we had a

Christian assembly every morning before lessons. I prayed and sang hymns, learning about religion and from religion. At eight years of age, learning about religion meant acquiring some kind of knowledge base. I didn't understand much, but that didn't seem to matter to Mr Thomas. All that was required of me was to know, in other words to *remember*, that Christians believed in God, went to church on the Sabbath, and read stories from the Bible about Abraham, Isaac, Jacob and others who once upon a time lived in exotic, far-off lands such as Israel and Egypt. Learning *from* religion was harder because we had to think about what all this was in aid of.

The school was well blessed, too, in being supported by a dedicated Board of Governors and a parental body that always showed a keen interest and involvement. Maybe it was this as much as anything that put me off liking it.

Mr Thomas went out of his way to try and make the atmosphere in his classroom positive and encouraging. Pupils' work was displayed on the walls, he made sure the wooden floor was buffed up to the nines, and there wasn't the tiniest piece of litter to be seen upon it. Litter was frowned upon by Mr Thomas. Graffiti wasn't invented, and even the most modern-minded of teachers would have dropped dead at the thought of children painting and scribbling on walls.

He always started and finished lessons on time and made a special point of never ignoring bad behaviour, even in the corridors and playground. There was a sense of community. The staff and pupils felt valued and respected. But not everybody came under the community umbrella; there were one or two outsiders who felt no commitment to the school.

The school was well run and orderly and related to the community it served, but it failed me personally in not having much influence on my behaviour. It would never have crossed my mind to physically attack Mr Thomas or any other teacher; children didn't do that sort of thing in my day. But offences were committed and my disruptions to lessons had a cumulative effect, making it harder and harder for Mr Thomas to teach and the other pupils to learn. I was sometimes over-active, walking around the classroom, flicking bits of paper or the silver tops of milk bottles at the other pupils, anything except concentrate on the work in hand.

I remember turning up for school one day with a shell in my pocket. It was of anti-aircraft proportions. The bullet section and the brass case were intact, but the explosive had been removed, so in the hands of a normal child it would have been quite harmless. I was sitting at the back of the class, and when Mr Thomas wasn't looking I pretended to Pearl Harbor him. I was holding on to the case firmly, yet the bullet part came loose and went whizzing over the heads of the other children. It missed its target by a couple of inches and slammed into the blackboard. I was sent to see the Headmaster and was caned.

On another occasion I persuaded the boy sitting next to me (I don't remember who it was, but I know it wasn't Jack Philips) to pull with his left hand the string of a plastic helicopter that I was holding with my right hand at sub-desk level. When the string was pulled the rotor blade detached from the hub, and on this occasion it flew, as intended, in the teacher's direction. It hovered next to his right ear as he wrote on the blackboard:

Friday 14th October 1955
Mathematics
Addition
58 = 42 +
60 = 53 +
71 = 60 +
95 = 8

He turned round quickly, but as we were very intently sitting facing the front, our identities were not given away as the rotor blade flopped on to his desk.

The following week I threw a dart into the calf of the boy sitting in front of me. Mr Thomas was away for some reason and the Headmaster was taking the class. On hearing the screams, he rushed over and was about to slap the wrong boy when I owned up with some urgency in my voice that I was the culprit.

I hate to admit it, but perhaps one thing I did learn as a child from being in care with so many other kids, is a code of honour. Whether or not I would have learned this, if I had remained with my mother in the East End, I don't know. It's an impossible question to answer. It's like asking if the dog would have caught the rabbit if the rabbit hadn't stopped running. Who knows?

At other times at school I was too introspective by far for an eight-year-old boy. I daydreamed, never did any work, and spent the lessons looking out of the window.

Perhaps this is why I haven't mentioned school until now; it was a non-entity. Mr Thomas moved me around, further away from the window into the middle of the classroom, to the front, the back of the classroom again, back to the window, but to no avail. My shutters were down most of the time and I only opened them if and when I wanted to; the amount of attention I gave to lessons was something I had control over. One of the most difficult times for me personally was when parents were allowed to attend the morning assembly. My sense of loss was made acute. I would look from the Assembly Hall window and the pull of the forest would be greater than ever, my extended departures into it at break- and lunch-times more frequent. The Essex County Council Education Committee's values were never really inculcated into me. There was no deal between us, no unwritten contract. I didn't really feel I belonged there. I would sit at my desk sometimes with my mouth open thinking back to Boyles Court, wondering why I had been sent there and why I had been taken away from my mother in the first place.

Today's dream was interrupted by the sound of my teacher's voice. 'Are you catching flies again, Denby? An angle of 90 degrees is usually called a right angle. They occur a great deal in the carpentered, man-made world. If you look around the room, you will see many examples of right angles.'

I looked around.

Huchinson had put his hand up. 'The corner, sir. The corner of the room; it is a right angle.'

'Good,' said Mr Thomas, pointing to the corner.

Ison had now put his hand up. 'The bookshelf, sir.'

'What about it?' asked Mr Thomas, stretching him.

'Where the line of the shelf meets the upright; that's 90 degrees.'

Mr Thomas pointed to Worthington. 'The tape recorder, sir; where the top meets the side.'

Mr Thomas went ahead and explained that an angle of less than 90 degrees is called an acute angle and an angle of size between 90 degrees and 180 degrees is known as an obtuse angle. He then picked up his cane and held it horizontally out in front of him. 'What sort of an angle is this?'

Even Huchinson couldn't answer this one.

Mr Thomas waited patiently, tapping the palm of his left hand with the cane. Ison scratched his head. I raised my hand and all eyes turned towards me.

'Go on then, Denby,' said Mr Thomas, pointing at me with the cane.

'It's a straight angle.'

Everybody laughed, except Mr Thomas. He was irritated. I'd

got it right for once. He stood there for a second, speechless. 'That's exactly what it is, a straight angle,' he said, when the hilarity had subsided sufficiently for his voice to be heard. Keeping his eyes on me, he then changed the subject and pointed quickly with his cane to the word 'Geometry' which was written on the blackboard. 'The name is derived from the Greek word *ge*, meaning "earth", and *metrein*, which is the verb "to measure". What's a verb?' The cane was now pointing at Rogers.

'A *doing* or *being* word, sir.'

'Yes, that will do,' said Mr Thomas.

I had distinguished myself by recognising and calling a straight angle exactly what it is, a straight angle. But there was no praise.

The day ended with me distinguishing myself again in a different, less admirable, way by getting into a fight.

Word went round during the last period of the afternoon that Philips had called me a 'dirty orphan' again and there was to be a showdown after school that day. I had inadvertently challenged Philips's ascribed superiority and status as best fighter in the class. If I won the tussle, the label would be transferred to me.

Philips and I had been sharing the same desk for a few days and I had the measure of him. I couldn't see what there was to be afraid of. He didn't look a weakling, but I suspected rightly he was a yellow-belly.

We had placed our chairs on desks and were waiting for the bell to go when I pre-empted the coming contest and threw ink in his face. I then punched him on the nose, leaving a firm, indelible ink print. He came at me and tried to get his foot behind my ankle. He wanted to push me over again, but I was wise to this strategy and I foiled him by grabbing his arm, turning my back towards him and throwing him over my shoulder on to the floor.

He rose to his feet, but then quickly backed off and began to cry.

I gained a great deal of respect from the other pupils, not least because Mr Thomas, sitting at the front of the class, saw everything and I didn't care whether he saw or not. The incident was sufficiently serious for the Headmaster to be called for. He told me off again, in no uncertain terms this time, and he caned me on both hands in front of the class. This attracted even more esteem from the other children and I was established as conquering hero.

We were steeped in a child-centred primary school culture and it showed in our behaviour. And I think at the same time I was afraid of school. Afraid of failing, knowing that I did not have the key to success. I think I was afraid of disappointing what I perceived to be anxious teachers, knowing at the same time that disappointing them was inevitable. The truth is I was bored a lot of the time because many of the things I was told to do in school were so trivial and made such limited demands on the spectrum of my talents. I was good at music, but nobody drew that out.

Andrew had a birthday present waiting for him on the breakfast table; a parcel from a philanthropist. We watched him open it. It was a clockwork steam engine. He then took a solitary card from its envelope, a simple wish for a happy birthday. I suggested that the train-set belonged to everybody, it was communal. The new engine was something we could all play with. Andrew seemed not to hear me and sat back in his chair admiring the engine, which he held up in front of him with both hands. Birthdays were important because for a day you were the centre of attention and most people were nice to you.

Betty and Patricia asked if they could leave the table, went to the flowerbeds and potted plants at the bottom of the garden, and picked a bunch of remainders as big as a football. Several minutes later, rushing back into the dining-room, they handed them over to Andrew. The cultivated roses, geraniums and white petunia mixed in with heather had all been growing by the creosoted fence at the side of the garden where the sun fell during the morning. He accepted the offering with a quick word of thanks. Instead of thinking how pleasant they would look in water, I thought how sissy flowers were.

I left for school with Andrew and Trevor and together we walked up Princess Lane and talked about the new engine and made plans to run it. This engine was attracting friends as though it were magnetic. Andrew knew we wanted him for his train. I arrived at school in a relatively good mood and it seemed to affect the whole class. We were all talking loudly when Mr Thomas, who said he had never heard such a racket, took the register.

I took my chewing-gum out of my mouth. It was a large amount, several big pieces masticated together with the remains of a strawberry-flavoured gobstopper.

'Hands on heads,' Mr Thomas ordered, looking at us in dismay and taking the cane from its corner.

I did as I was told, same as everybody, but the chewing-gum was still in the palm of my hand and it stuck fast to the top of my head, setting hard as I waited for the command to take hands down. When the word came it was too late, the chewing-gum was left matted in my hair like a pink cowpat on dry grass.

Mr Thomas put his cane away and began calling out our names. 'Andrews.'

'Yes, sir.'

'Bellingham.'

'Yes, sir.'

'Bradley.'

'Yes, sir.'

'Croydon.'

'Yes, sir.'

When he came to me, Mr Thomas, on the spur of the moment, for some reason best known to himself, pronounced my name 'Denbeye' instead of 'Denby'. He had never pronounced my name like this before. I replied instantly with an archaic, 'Yes, sire!' My timing was perfect. I got a loud laugh and I wasn't even trying.

Mr Thomas couldn't help smiling himself. I was learning that if you want to be funny, timing is everything.

At playtime I ran into the playground pulling at the tangled mess of chewing-gum in my hair. The soft September sun on my head was enough to harden the gum, and it was obviously going to take more than a few tugs with the fingers to remove it. After school, I cut it out with a penknife and half-scalped myself in the process. I was now left with a large bald patch which I showed to Barry.

'Auntie Blodwen'll take exception if she sees that,' he said. 'Whatever you do, *don't* let her brush your hair in the morning, what's left of it.'

The next day in the natural science lesson, Mr Thomas happened to look up and noticed me staring out of the classroom window. He must have wondered what was going on inside my head.

'Get on with your work, Denby,' he ordered, in his thick, Welsh accent.

These were the days when there was no National Curriculum

and a great deal of teaching was done on a whole-class basis. The pupils all tackled the same task while the teacher sat at the front and read a book. I surfaced from my daydream of kings and queens in steam machines.

Mr Thomas came over to my desk intent on looking through my work-book and reproaching me. I spoke first. 'Why can't we learn about steam engines? That's science, innit?'

'Yes,' said Mr Thomas. 'But why do you want to learn about steam engines? Do you want to be a train driver when you grow up?'

'I thought it would be interesting, that's all. What makes them go?'

Mr Thomas was turning the pages of my work-book and shaking his head in disbelief as he answered my question. 'The successive expansion and rapid condensation of steam . . .'

I made no serious attempt to settle down at school and Mr Thomas had reached his wits' end. He was seemingly forever going on at me about school rules and about having the right equipment. I had been caned and slapped. The rod had not been spared. It was an age that still reckoned sparing the rod would spoil the child. It was prudent to chastise and correct a child forcefully. I'd had a what-for, several fourpenny ones, and was left with thick ears. The other boys in my class were such little gentlemen by comparison, well behaved and nicely spoken teacher's pets and goody two shoes. I think they were happier than me. My bad behaviour and larking about were still hiding-places for sadness.

Mr Thomas spoke to me one day on the football pitch. I was lethargic during the game, walking after the ball instead of running with it. I defended the position of left back. There were no goals, yet plenty of near-misses at my end, the ball hitting the post a number of times. Mr Thomas always said my team would be better off without me – if I were 'left back' in the dressing-room or 'right back' behind the goal post.

When the action was safely at the other end of the pitch, he asked what was going on inside my head. Why wasn't I learning a satisfactory amount of what I was supposed to be learning? Was I unhappy?

What a question! I shrugged my shoulders and looked down at the grass. Then in one of those rare moments when a schoolteacher gets really close to a pupil, Mr Thomas answered his own question. 'You don't know what happiness is, do you?'

I was embarrassed and burrowed with the heel of my boot into the ground. 'Do you think there's going to be a war?' I asked, changing the subject.

'No,' he said.

'Why is England making bigger and bigger hydrogen bombs?'

'Government policy.'

'It would be a good idea if the superpowers scaled down their hoards of weapons and spent more money on hospitals and schools,' I said. 'Is it true, sir, that an atom bomb could wipe out the whole of London and the Home Counties?'

'Get back to your position.'

'Is it true that a hydrogen bomb produces more radioactive fall-out than an atom bomb?'

'Get back to your position.'

'Why?'

'Because your goal is being attacked.'

The ball bounced its way back to our end of the field and I went after it. Mr Thomas watched me go.

My head was flooded with ideas of nuclear destruction. For once, I saved the ball and sent it like a guided missile across to Paul Worthington on the right wing. Paul started off in speedy fashion, soon made a pass to the centre, and the ball was slammed home by Ison. Three minutes later a Huchinson corner was headed in by Philips and the score was an unbelievable 2–0 to my team. The other side fought back and four minutes before the interval the arrears were reduced with a penalty. Our goalie hadn't a chance in hell of saving it. It was of the unstoppable variety.

There were reports that Russia had tested another hydrogen bomb, the world's most powerful weapon. Details were scarce about the actual effects of the explosion and much was left to the imagination. My imagination was vivid.

My brain was also clogged with information about kings and queens, ambitious generals, brave sailors and the Cape of Good Hope. Twelve twelves are one hundred and forty something and there are two hundred and forty pence in £1? What I would have given for a decimal system.

On my way to school I passed row upon row of expensive houses. They were all at the height of demand for aspiring young couples at a time when the clamour to own one's home was gathering momentum. On my way home from school I sang with the other boys from Gibblings Shaw:

We are some of the Gibblings, we are some of the boys.
We know our manners, we spend our tanners. We are
    some of the boys.

And then to the tune of 'Colonel Bogey's March':

Hitler has only got one ball. Rommel has two,
    but very small.
Himmler is very similar. But poor old Goebbels
    has no balls at all.

When we arrived back at the children's home we watched *The Flower Pot Men* on television. We still only had one channel, BBC. But we were aware of ITV, this other station that was inside the box and yet somehow not inside it. We envied the children at school who had commercial television and access to advertisements for Gibbs toothpaste, and the loquacious Hughie Green who could 'double your money' if you answered the most mundane of questions correctly, or even incorrectly come to that. We watched television, had our tea, played in the playroom, then went to bed.

Next morning when I came down to breakfast Auntie Blodwen was standing at the bottom of the stairs with her hands behind her back, legs slightly apart. The only thing missing was a Gestapo guard dog. The Irish setter would never do, she was too docile, asleep even now in her basket. I had my breakfast and left for school, somewhat bothered by Auntie Blodwen's posturing. During morning break I wandered so far off into the woods that it took me twenty minutes to get back. Mr Thomas's face twisted into a shocked expression as I wandered back into the classroom, hands in pockets, at eleven-twenty.

'It won't do, Denby,' he said. 'Here we are in the middle of a rehearsal and you barge in from nowhere . . .' His exasperation grew and left him speechless. I picked up my guitar, bewildered by his outburst, and began to play.

The management of my emotional and behavioural difficulties was a continuous source of anguish for Mr Thomas. He did not know how to provide for me. The problem was as old as education itself and I guess never far from his mind.

We were rehearsing a rock 'n' roll performance. My first instrument was a home-made guitar, my second was my voice. American rock 'n' roll with its implied subversion was barely acceptable socially and was soon to be banned by the BBC's

Light programme, but we succeeded in having our group for the time being, and all signs of self-consciousness faded as I lowered my chin, gritted my teeth, and brutally knocked out 'Rock Around the Clock' on my acoustic guitar, while Rogers and Ison harmonised on mouth organ and sax and Huchinson plucked a bass.

Mr Carr came into the classroom to listen to our efforts. The memory of the fight I'd had with Philips was still with him and the look he gave me as he came through the door was simply one of hostility. He soon looked away and began heaping praise on the other members of the group. I suspected he was jealous and secretly wanted to play guitar himself – or at least wear one around his neck.

As we practised, the Headmaster took Mr Thomas to one side and, between concentrating on my chord changes, I noticed Mr Thomas nodding his head.

There was an indispensable extra rehearsal after school with Mr Thomas, and before we began we had another disagreement as to whether or not Bill Haley could really sing and play the guitar.

'Anyway, Denby,' Mr Thomas said, 'that's neither here nor there. Mr Carr has decided that you are not to play in the group any longer. He wants you to concentrate harder on your written work first. If that improves and if there's a change for the better in your behaviour, you might be allowed back in. And, to be honest, I can't help thinking that Mr Carr is right.'

Although bitterly disappointed, I wasn't that surprised. I was used to my world crashing down around me. I protested, nevertheless. 'Who's going to replace me?'

'Jack Philips,' Mr Thomas said. 'He's a good player, quite frankly, and he owns a proper guitar.'

'Yeah, but can he sing?' I asked quietly, lowering my head and undoing the guitar strap.

So it was all a pretext. My lack of application to schoolwork and my bad behaviour had nothing to do with being thrown out of the group. Philips was better than me and he had a better guitar.

My experience of school was out of the ordinary. It was expected that I and other children like me would never achieve much artistically or academically. There was always a barrier between my teachers and me. As I grew older, the realisation that I couldn't *do* anything and was always bottom of the class began to matter. I began to realise deep down that I might leave school one day barely able to read or write.

That evening, Jenny, who had been waiting for me and sleeping flat on her stomach in the scullery, welcomed me as I went through the side door. I patted her gently and she reciprocated by licking my legs, the bits around the knees between the long socks and short trousers. I looked down at her, thinking I had one friend at least.

In bed, lying awake, I took a halting breath and wiped a last tear from my face. My needs were many, personal, social and educational, but there was nobody agonising over what would be best for me. I was much more vulnerable than a typical schoolboy. What I needed more than anything was a warm, supportive relationship with somebody. Leaving my own bed, I crept silently across the landing to Patricia's room.

7

Home for a Day

Something had been going on behind the scenes. I was informed that I was going home to visit my mother, on Sunday.

'There's something else you need to know,' Auntie Blodwen said, sitting opposite me in the office. 'Your mother has married, again. His name is Joseph Smith. You have a stepfather.'

Auntie Agnes was at Auntie Blodwen's side, as usual, backing up her every word and nodding in agreement.

'I thought Fishy was my father,' I said.

Auntie Blodwen looked at me hard for a second before replying. 'Who or what the bloomin' heck is Fishy?'

'He used to come to the flat and clean the windows,' I said.

Auntie Blodwen rolled her eyes around the room and Auntie Agnes followed her lead. 'Fishy,' said Auntie Blodwen, pointedly, 'or whatever his name is, may or may not be your father. You may never know who your real father is, you were born out of wedlock, you little bastard, but you now have a stepfather and what's important is that you are going to meet him on Sunday.'

'I don't want to,' I said.

'It has nothing to do with what you want or what you don't want,' Auntie Agnes said.

My mother had married a man I had never heard of or met. I had not so much as been invited to the wedding and now I was to be presented to him and him to me. Why? When I came face to face with him, how was I supposed to react? And how would he react to me? I began to be afraid.

On the day, Miss Abbott came and collected me in her car. I sat in the back in my Sunday clothes, with my hair brushed neatly under my school cap. She took me home by the back streets as far as she could to avoid the traffic, and on the way openly complimented herself and the system on what she perceived to be my changed attitude and demeanour. 'My! What a change there is. Your mother won't recognise you.'

I began to feel awkward as we neared the end of our journey and, sure enough, the neighbours stopped and stared at me as the car pulled up outside The Buildings. I stepped out, immaculately groomed, not a hair out of place. My tie was adjusted and a macintosh folded neatly over my arm.

And Miss Abbott carried her head in a haughty fashion, too. 'What is this?' she said, looking up at The Buildings and shaking her head. 'An army barracks or a prison complex?'

She was right. The Buildings imposed themselves upon everybody and everything. If she herself lived in one of those Victorian terraces, the kind that I saw every day now on my way to school, The Buildings would have seemed vast in breadth and height and appallingly grey by comparison. We entered the tenement block and climbed the stairs.

At the front door to the flat, Miss Abbott fleetingly told my mother that she would be back at six o'clock, then left me there without another word.

The pane of glass was still missing from the door, but a piece of wood had been nailed across the hole to stop the draught along the passage. My mother answered the door. There was a strong smell of cooked or cooking food coming from the scullery. I followed her along the passage and into the front room. The atmosphere was overheated and the limited space more crowded than ever with patriotic ornamentation and, lo and behold, a television. A panicked cockroach fell from the blank screen as we entered the room.

'You should be used to that sort of thing,' my mother said, noticing my reaction.

'Not any more I'm not,' I replied.

She looked humiliated, and I could tell that the way I was dressed seemed to irritate her too. She kept looking me up and down.

I think she'd also got used to me not being around and resented having to be there for me. We didn't talk in a meaningful way. It was evident that something had come between us.

I wasn't sure how to respond to my mother because I was changing as a person without her being there to influence the change. With my new surroundings at the children's home, I was in no man's land and caught between two cultural identities. I wasn't sure which identity was mine: the East End home port, or the children's home.

I was given nothing to do so I looked out of the window. As the day wore on, nothing was said about my new stepfather and I was grateful for that and for his absence. My mother was still taking an interest in the piano and going through her own little renaissance period, getting to grips with old, half-forgotten melodies. I listened to her play for a while then, behind her back, crept downstairs and went outside. The neighbours looked me up and down and called me 'Little Lord Muck' to my face. I pretended to them that I liked my clothes, but I would have liked to have snatched the cap from my head and thrown it down for them to trample on.

When I went back to the flat my new stepfather was there, asleep in Fishy's armchair, smelling strongly of beer. I noticed he only had one leg and one eye and then I saw the crutches lying across the settee.

My mother introduced him to me as he slept, saying that his name was Joe and that he was working. This was always the first thing to be established round The Buildings, whether a person had a job or not. Joe was a public lavatory attendant, my mother informed me.

'His toilet is in Stratford Broadway,' she said.

I knew the Broadway to be surrounded by pubs so I imagined he had lots of visitors. I was curious about the leg and the eye, the ones that were missing, and my mother told me that the leg had been crushed after a tree trunk had spun off a lorry, taking Joe with it, and the eye had been lost on the end of a bottle.

'Do you want some dinner?' my mother asked. 'Joe's had his.'

When he woke up, Joe seemed on the face of it to accept me as a stepson unconditionally, perceiving no threat from me, I suppose. I was an absent stepson so the relationship would not be stressed. For the moment, however, the conversation was forced. The truth is, he had nothing of interest to say.

He said he was going to have a 'slash' and he reached across for his crutches. Pulling himself up on to them, he swung himself along to the toilet at the end of the passage and relieved himself.

Returning to the front room, he sat down to read. *The News of the World* was his choice of linen. He produced some comics that were tucked inside the newspaper and I sat down immediately opposite him, to read the *Dandy* and the *Beano*. Auntie Blodwen wouldn't entertain the *Dandy* or the *Beano* at Gibblings Shaw, perceiving them to be, at best, of no educational value and, at worst, common. Auntie Blodwen's choice for us was *The Children's Newspaper*, so the comics were a real treat.

Spoilt

It was humiliating for me to visit and for my mother and stepfather to be visited. It was a sad, sad arrangement that we all felt uncomfortable with. We were fulfilling an obligation. Loving was impossible.

My mother and stepfather didn't remember to ask what it was like at the home, what I had done at school, or even how I was getting on in more general terms. They knew nothing about the existence of the Irish setter; didn't know its name, or that it had smooth hair and was unexcitable by nature. They had never heard the dog bark. My mother and stepfather weren't aware of the two cats, the ginger one and the grey one. They didn't know that the rabbit's name was Sally or where she slept. They had never stroked Sally as I had done and tentatively picked her up. They didn't know where I slept, had not made my bed, or done any of the other small things that parents do in the course of a childhood. They had never been inside my bedroom. They had never been inside the house; did not know what it smelled like, that it smelled of Wilton carpet. They had never tasted Auntie Gladys's disgusting trifle. They did not know that I'd had a fight with Jack Philips and been thrown out of the rock 'n' roll group at school; they were not aware that I was caned at school and beaten at the children's home with fists, shoes that were still attached to feet, rulers, canes and hairbrushes. Not one visit paid, to my school or to Gibblings Shaw.

She handed me another comic as I sat on the edge of the armchair, my back as straight as a classical guitar player.

'Who is my *real* dad?' I asked, looking intently at the pictures of the Bash Street kids in the comic as though the fiction were more real than my own genealogy. The characters guzzled and chomped 'Yahoo, Yahoo!' from the pages. This was decades before the internet was even dreamed of.

My mother pretended to laugh. 'He was killed in the war.'

'How? What happened to him?' I looked up at the same moment as my stepfather. He was as surprised to hear this as I was.

There was more laughter from my mother to allay the lie. 'Your old man was drowned,' she said. 'His ship was torpedoed by a German submarine.' She went to the sink in the scullery and noisily started some washing-up. My stepfather put his newspaper down and pursued her along the passage on his crutches.

'Wow', I thought, still flicking through the pages of the comic with a bandaged finger. A German submarine! It didn't occur to me that my real father couldn't have died before I was conceived. What my mother told me was a very feeble untruth, but it had me fooled for years. I went into the scullery.

'Couldn't he get off the ship before it sank?'

'He did,' my mother invented. 'He jumped into the water and was drowned. I've told you.' A hint of impatience had crept into her voice.

'Couldn't he swim?'

'No,' she said. 'He couldn't. Go back into the front room. I'm trying to do this washing-up.'

I returned to the front room with my comic. She was beginning to raise her voice and I felt sad again.

Tim, the half-brother whom I hadn't seen since he had, without warning, left Gibblings Shaw, let himself in through the front door. He was home from visiting his girlfriend in one of the other blocks of flats. Hardly knowing each other, we both felt shy and uncomfortable alone in the front room.

He went into the scullery and joined my mother and stepfather. He then left without saying goodbye.

A sandwich was brought in to me by my mother and I ate it standing at the table. When I had finished, my mother came back into the front room, sat down, and had her sandwich. Joe sat down again in the armchair and ate his with a dishcloth over his leg. It would have been asking too much to sit at the table as a family.

My half-sister, Mavis, on a Sunday visit, let herself into the flat and joined us in the front room. She had her son Jim with her. He was the same age as me, and it felt strange to be an uncle to someone my own age. Mavis helped herself to tea, and Jim and I watched *Robin Hood* on the television. It was turned up very loud and the grown-ups talked over the reverberation of sounds about Tim's coming marriage to a girl called Iris.

I lent an ear to the conversation. Tim was going to live with Iris and her parents in their flat in one of the tenement blocks in Belmont Road. I interrupted and told everybody about Sally, the black rabbit, and how I had to remember to give her carrots and cabbage every morning before school and clean her hutch out every other day after school.

'It was all right at first,' I said, 'but I'm getting a bit fed up with it now. She bit my finger.' I held out my hand and showed them my bandaged finger that they hadn't even noticed.

It was almost time to return to Gibblings Shaw, so I gathered my comics together into a neat pile on the table and then went along the passage to the toilet. Things had taken a turn for the better; there was a roll of proper toilet paper standing next to the lavatory pan. It was the shiny kind, not very efficacious; it had 'London County Council' written all over it in blue ink, but at least it was toilet paper.

At six o'clock sharp, Miss Abbott came to collect me. I was relieved that she didn't ask to come in. I felt so ashamed of the smell and untidiness of the place. Jim went halfway along the passage to get a look at her and my stepfather and Mavis remained in the front room as I was handed over by my mother.

Home for a Day

On the way back in the car it started to rain and a sadness came over me again. Miss Abbott said very little, concentrating instead on the road ahead, peering intently over and under the windscreen wipers as they splashed from side to side. Sooner than expected, the car drew up outside Gibblings Shaw and we ran out of the rain into the house as my mind turned to other things and places. I hurried into the playroom and hid my comics in my locker while Miss Abbott gave an account of the day's events to Auntie Blodwen in the hall.

I made one or two further visits to my mother and stepfather, always on the second Sunday of the month. It was always the same routine. My mother would play the piano while I wandered around outside in the road, my stepfather would return from the pub smelling of beer, Mavis would pop in with Jim for a cup of tea, and Tim would pop in, either with Iris or on his own. I wondered about Fishy and whose windows he was cleaning. Then suddenly, without any explanation, I was stopped from visiting.

8

School Holidays

Henry was leaving. It was the end of term, he was fifteen, and it was time to go out into the big wide world. He had expressed an interest in the Army and was now going to be a soldier; he was moving from one institution to another. There was no point, apparently, in his staying on at school, not even until the end of the academic year. His leaving school may not have been legal, but that's the way it was.

It also happened to be Betty's birthday, and at her place on the Big table was a present wrapped up for her. She opened it. It was a sewing set: a small case with a pair of scissors, needles and a thimble. We sang happy birthday and then I sang it a second time, changing the words:

> Happy birthday to you,
> I went to the zoo.
> I saw a great big monkey
> And it looked just like you.

There was applause, then Auntie Blodwen kicked in with her usual lament: 'You've all got to go sometime. And anyway,' she added, 'with Henry's council flat mentality, the Army is the best place for him. Now get on with eating your breakfast, and remember that lots of children don't have any.'

Life went on without Henry: the Christmas holiday and the domesticity of the home, sitting up at the dining-room tables or watching television in the office (it was a brand-new Ferguson, the latest model, and we watched David Whitfield singing in Italian *Santo Natale*). We played with new Dinky toys, and Meccano, had nativity stories read to us, ate sweets and cleaned our teeth with new toothbrushes and, if we were lucky, Gibbs toothpaste.

After Christmas, I woke very early one Sunday morning and decided to switch the fire-alarm on. The switch was on the wall at the bottom of the stairs. For six long seconds bells rang out all over the house until Auntie Blodwen got to the switch. I had counted the seconds. She was getting quicker.

I went to the nearest bathroom and, as I washed, I looked out of the open window above the sink into the back garden. Huge snowflakes were falling and the settling white downy made the trees look so peaceful. I was familiar with the trees now and knew all their names. The one closest to the house was a crab-apple; the one straight ahead was a sycamore; and the very tall one at the bottom of the garden was a silver birch.

I looked down and watched the water from the tap disappear down the plughole while I brushed my teeth. The water seemed to blink back at me as it reflected the room's light before vanishing into what was for me the dark unknown. The pipes and tubes kept me guessing. Who knew where they led to? Somewhere secret. I would have stayed longer observing the phenomenon of the sink's blinking eye, but I had to get ready for church, a Communion service for which we had prepared ourselves by silent confession in the office the night before, asking pardon for our sins and, encouraged by Auntie Blodwen, searching for some meaning in our lives. Our Sunday lunch was left in a low oven to finish cooking.

Spiritually unmoved by the Communion service and still in a state, Auntie Blodwen led us down the hill and back to Gibblings Shaw. In the dining-room, Auntie Agnes raised the lid of the meat casserole. An emetic blend of smells poured out from the economical hotpot, a one-dish meal. Auntie Agnes went round the tables and ladled out the lamb and onions, while through the service hatch we all listened to *The Billy Cotton Band Show* on the wireless set.

'A family that eats together stays together,' Auntie Agnes said.

Her maxim was that mealtimes are basic for the unity of families, but the reality was that, in this dining-room, none of us wanted to be there.

After lunch I went upstairs with Trevor to play. Pop returned to the sick-room from the free lunch he had shared with us and continued tapping away on his typewriter. We could hear the tap, tap, tap as we played. Pop was aware of us next door, but he always kept himself to himself. On this particular Sunday he came into the dormitory to complain about the noise we were making, so we went downstairs.

In the playroom, Trevor and I set up a makeshift table tennis table and began to play: 1–Nil. 2–Nil. 2–1. 3–1. 4–1. 2–4. 3–4. 3–5. As the score mounted, my voice lifted too: 16–12. 17–12. 18–12.

Just then, Pop came through from the hall on his way to the boot room; '18–12,' he echoed. 'Tchaikovsky's Overture. Don't need the cannons. There's enough ear-splitting noise.'

Again, I wondered what he meant. The grown-ups had a knack of coming out with the most puzzling, incomprehensible statements.

Trevor beat me fair and square and, after a return game, we went outside into the garden.

Above our heads the branches of the birch and sycamore were stooping under the weight of snow. Trevor and I got to work and built a snowman in the middle of the covered lawn.

We heaped together enough snow for the body with our bare hands, shaping it as we went.

And then, starting off with a small ball of snow, we skilfully rolled this around the garden, backwards and forwards, until it was characteristic of a life-size head. There was an art to making the small ball of snow grow bigger and bigger by rolling it around. The grown-ups couldn't do it. The secret was never to use fresh snow, but to wait at least a day or night until the fall had settled. It then had density and would cohere. Fresh snow was too fluffy and would not bond.

After a count of three we lifted the head on to the body and stuck a carrot in it to represent a nose, and inserted pebbles for the eyes. The gardener-cum-handyman had left an old hat and a scarf in the boiler-room, so we borrowed them. Pop, feeling guilty I suppose because he had thrown us out of our dormitory, contributed a walking-stick and one of his pipes. I stuck the walking-stick in the snow a foot from the white brute and then leaned the crook against the right side of the body. I stuck Pop's pipe in its face: I made quite a point of it, and then with a finger I forced a smile. A serried rank of onions was sunk into the front of its body and, with this final touch, the snowman seemed to come to life. *It* became *he*, and *he* was wearing a white overcoat with onion buttons.

We stood back to admire our work. We couldn't help but feel proud of *him*. The background of a clear blue sky made the snowman look a picture.

Auntie Blodwen stole a glance from an upstairs window. She didn't want anything to do with it, but was drawn back to the window as if by an invisible thread. The snowman was *that* good, even though I say so myself.

Christine ran out of the house and Andrew ran out after her. Soon there was a group surrounding the snowman like a panel of judges, and Trevor and I stood next to *him* and soaked up the praise.

The following morning we rushed to a window to get a look at him. He'd been decimated. His hat and scarf were gone and his head knocked off, his body beaten with the very stick he used to stand up with. We guessed Auntie Blodwen was the murderer and, with super-childlike resilience, we tried to put our grief behind us.

Then the new term was on top of us and we were back at school. And, before we knew it, the weather broke and we were on holiday again, out of an overcrowded classroom.

As a nine-year-old I took the different experiences of school life on holiday with me, unable to shake it off altogether; the memory of Mr Thomas, rock 'n' roll performances, football matches and the names I was called, they all stayed with me. My grief at losing the snowman was almost behind me now and my mourning for loss of home and family, such as it was, put on hold. I tried to cope with all the emotions that were coming in at me. I would let them all out again in due time. At least my mother was still alive, even if I had lost her. Not like the snowman. And as for Patricia's mother – she had killed herself leaping from a third-floor window. There had been an attempt at concealment, but Patricia wasn't stupid. I made a brave effort at psychologically trying to put my grief behind me, but I couldn't control my physical state.

I became unwell and was put to bed. Pop was away, so I was laid up in the sick-room. The doctor came and probed around in search of something; first the nose, then the throat and the ears. He withdrew his otoscope. 'It would help enormously if you washed inside your ears from time to time,' he said, pricking my thumb with a needle.

After he'd gone, I stretched my legs and looked out of the closed window to the garden below. Violets demurred and reclined shyly behind green leaves as if they knew I was watching, and even the road beyond ran away from me. I hated being by myself and my legs were so stiff from lying in bed. My thoughts turned to my new stepfather. I remembered how he smelled of beer and I mused over his missing left eye. The lid, I recalled, was swallowed up by the socket and this left a hollow in that side of the face. I tried to imitate my stepfather's facial expression. I needed to find a way of closing my eye without screwing my face up. Before long I found I could do it, and then I hopped around the room on one leg, maintaining a permanent blink in one eye. But I soon tired of that, returned to my bed, and looked forward to the cleaner tidying the room and punctuating my day. She always talked and did her best to cheer me up.

She came again and we chatted. Before she left I looked at her with one eye closed and she gave me a strange look of her own. Maintaining my stare, I made her laugh and extracted a promise to come back later.

When I thought she had forgotten, I called out. 'Auntie Maxwell. Auntie Maxwell.'

She returned and looked down on me in my bed, clutching her yellow duster in her hand.

'What are you plaguing me for now?' she asked.

'Tell me about the old days again.'

'Not until you've finished drinking that medicine. You'll never get better if you don't take it.' She stood watching over me. Her expression was pleasant and she wore a royal-blue apron, exactly the same shade as the Bible in the glass-fronted cabinet in the office, I recollect, but without the gold inlay. I unscrambled myself from the bedclothes and finished what was left in the bottom of the glass as she turned for the door. 'The old days,' I insisted.

'Well now,' she said, turning and pretending to dust Pop's typewriter. 'When I was your age . . .'

'That will be enough, Auntie Maxwell.' Auntie Blodwen had appeared in the doorway. 'The boy will settle down just as soon as you leave.'

Auntie Maxwell left like a thief in the night as Auntie Blodwen quickly surveyed the room with her eyes and then followed Auntie Maxwell downstairs. I rose cautiously, went out on to the landing, and moved as close to the top of the stairs as I thought it was safe to do, looking for company. There was none, until eight o'clock when the other children started coming up, and frightened me back to bed with stories of nuclear destruction. I prayed:

Lord, keep us safe this night, secure from all our fears.
May angels guard us while we sleep, till morning light
    appears?

By about ten o'clock, I had dropped off to sleep, but now I lay uncomfortably wide awake. My unused clothes were still neatly folded on Pop's chair and Enid Blyton was on top of the pile. I buried my face in the pillow. There were few tears left to cry. As I pushed the cool linen against my eyes, schemes of vengeance, aimed at Auntie Blodwen and children who frightened me, flashed through my mind. I did not even halt at the thought of burning the house down.

In a day or two I recovered sufficiently for them to let me get up and I went out with George and Trevor for the afternoon. Together we sauntered down the lane that ran behind Gibblings Shaw and continued towards Lady Linda's field. Lady Linda was a member of the local landed gentry and lived with her husband in a large property that boasted stables and a swimming-pool. We often trespassed on their land: playing, climbing trees, helping ourselves to fruit from the orchard and sharing it with the horses. As we came to the stile, distant church bells pealed the half-hour. We climbed over the stile and entered the field, running immediately down its gentle slope towards the stables.

The ground became more even, the sound of the church bells fading as we ran. Our faces were red and we were breathless when we reached the enclosure. To our left, partly hidden by the stable wall, we noticed a small tent near the swimming-pool. There were two boys in front of the tent, cooking over a wood-burning fire. It was two of Father Worthington's boys. He was a friend of Lady Linda, so it was no surprise to see his children on her land. We walked over to them. Our meeting was friendly, and Michael and Paul shared what they had to eat with us.

On an impulse, I picked up *The Children's Newspaper* that was lying in front of the tent, rolled it into a tube, and lit the end from the campfire. I then went chasing across the field with it held above my head, whooping at the top of my voice. Trevor and George followed, adding to the disruption, but Michael and Paul restrained themselves in a way that was expected of a priest's children at the time. They stood aghast in front of the tent. What if Lady Linda saw the fiasco from a window?

The next thing I knew, smoke was wafting over the roof of the stables. Running through the open-plan building, I had mindlessly set light to the hay stacked on top of the rafters of the low ceiling. I stopped dead in my tracks. 'Oh, no,' I whispered, throwing *The Children's Newspaper* to the ground and stamping on it with my foot.

Sir William and Lady Linda only had two horses, a prizewinning mare named Marilyn and a stallion called Roger, but at that moment it was two too many. The horses were inside the stables. By the time George and Trevor had caught up with me, the smoke was dense and the horses were whinnying. George stood there, thoughtfully looking up, as though we had all the time in the world.

But Trevor was running up and down and round in circles. 'Find a bucket!' he shouted. 'Quick.'

'We'll need more than a bucket,' I said, looking up at the smoke that was beginning to billow. 'Shouldn't we let Marilyn and Roger out first?'

'We haven't got time,' Trevor said. 'We can put it out if we hurry. We can fetch water from the horses' drinking trough, but we need some buckets.'

I prayed quietly that Trevor was right. If the fire went out of control and the stables burned down, I was done for. Auntie Blodwen would have my life. I suddenly felt weak at the thought of what she would do to me. The horses whinnied louder and louder and I felt for them, understanding their fear.

Michael and Paul were suddenly standing beside us breathless, arms akimbo.

'There are buckets in the shed!' Michael shouted, 'but let's get the horses out first.'

'Fuck the horses,' Trevor said. 'Fetch some buckets.'

'Fuck you, too,' Michael said.

Trevor and I stopped running round in circles and looked at Michael for a second. We hadn't expected such vocabulary from the vicar's son.

'I'm letting the horses out,' Michael confirmed. 'And fetch water from the swimming-pool, you pair of consummate wallies. There's not enough in the horses' drinking trough to drown a rat.'

'Let Marilyn and Roger out, then!' I screamed at him. 'I can see flames up there.'

It was true; somewhere inside the billowing white smoke there was an ominous orange patch and a crackling sound. Marilyn and Roger were starting to kick.

'Follow me,' Paul said, running out of the stables. 'I'll show you where the buckets are.'

We ran out of the stables after Paul to the shed on the other side of the paddock, only to discover that the door was locked with a padlock.

'We'll have to break it open,' Trevor said.

'Dare we?' Paul asked.

'Oh, shut up,' I said.

We were stumped. I watched over my shoulder as the horses galloped out into the paddock – Michael had let them out. Once they had put some distance between themselves and the stables, they were seemingly unconcerned that their house was burning down and they had started to graze.

At least they were safe. Just as I had this thought, I noticed an old rosette lying on the ground, an award maybe, that Marilyn had won and then lost. It was lying upside down and was made of blue ribbon. But, more interestingly, on its back was a large, rusty old pin. I picked the rosette up and poked the thin end of the pin into the keyhole of the padlock. With a few deft turns, I had the padlock in the position that I wished to have it, hanging from the staple on the right side of the hasp. We opened the door, found a bucket each, and headed for the swimming-pool. Smoke was rising as we headed back to the stables with our buckets of water. I discovered very quickly how heavy water is.

Most of it landed on our heads as we threw it up into the flames. So then it was back to the swimming-pool at full speed for another draught.

By the time I had returned with my second bucket, Lady Linda's handyman was up a small ladder against the side of the building. In his loose clothes and tight belt, I could see it was the same man who sometimes came to Gibblings Shaw to cut the grass and generally put things right. I met him halfway and handed my bucket of water to him.

Through the open-ended wall of the building he threw the water on top of the tightly stacked bales of straw and it seeped down. This had the desired effect; there was extra smoke, but the flames died down.

'The fire brigade is on its way,' the handyman said, handing me back my bucket. 'But I think it's under control now. Thank God for this damp weather, otherwise you and the horses might have been in real trouble. Fetch another bucket of water, will you, please? Just in case.'

When I returned with my third bucket, Lady Linda was in the paddock with the horses. A police car pulled up in the lane and, with a wave of the hand, Lady Linda beckoned to the driver.

The policemen drove the car into the paddock and, after a few words with Lady Linda, the taller of the two policemen called me over to where he was now standing. I handed my last bucket of water up to the handyman and went as bidden. Michael and Paul were already standing in front of the policemen, and George and Trevor left their buckets of water at the foot of the ladder and joined us.

'Who struck the match?' the tall policeman asked.

'He did.' My so-called friends were all pointing at me.

'No I didn't,' I said. 'I haven't got any fucking matches. What are you all pointing at me for?' I looked at Michael and Paul. 'You struck the match.'

'Yes, of course we did,' Michael said. 'We struck the match to start a fire to cook our tea on, but we didn't start *the fire*.'

'Strictly speaking,' Paul said to his brother, 'it was you who struck the match. You lit the fire, not me.'

'Well, yes, I know, but . . .'

'What's your name?' the shorter policeman asked Michael.

'My father is the vicar,' he replied.

'I don't care if he's Rocky Marciano. What's your name?'

At that point we were all distracted by the fire-engine as it pulled into the paddock, bell ringing. The fire was out, but the firemen unrolled a thin hose and doused the whole building down, inside and out, with a fine spray of water.

The handyman came over and joined us as the tall policeman turned to Lady Linda. 'Is your husband at home, Lady Linda?'

'No,' she said. 'He's in Monaco. But I gave permission for Michael and Paul, Father Worthington's sons, to camp here, and I told them they could have a wood-fire.'

'I see,' said the policeman. 'It is cold for the month of May.'

'Exactly,' said Lady Linda. 'I think you'll find that these boys from Gibblings Shaw are probably to blame for the stables' fire.' She made a slight gesture with a wizened hand towards George, Trevor and me.

'You're from Gibblings Shaw, are you?' the tall policeman asked, looking at us again, this time with an eyebrow raised.

'Yes,' I said, owning up at the same time to the fact that I was responsible for lighting a rolled-up newspaper and dashing into the stables.

'Will you be wanting to press charges, Lady Linda?' the policeman asked.

Lady Linda looked at me. 'That will depend on my husband,' she said. 'He will have to decide when he returns home.'

'When will that be, Lady Linda?'

'Friday,' she said. 'Thank goodness the horses weren't inside.'

'They were inside,' George said.

The Worthington boys bowed their heads in shame and wandered off across the field. Lowering their tent, they abandoned camp.

The police took George, Trevor and me back to Gibblings Shaw in the back of their Wolseley, and on the way I contemplated what was in store for me.

Auntie Blodwen answered the front door. 'I should have known,' she said. 'I heard the fire-engine go by. What have they done?'

The tall policeman explained and Auntie Blodwen looked at me in a way she had never done before. There was a paragon look of evil in her eyes.

'What happens next,' said the shorter policeman, 'depends on whether or not Lady Linda wants to press charges. If she does, something as serious as this could go a long way.'

As soon as the policemen left I was locked in the cellar on my own. Auntie Blodwen almost threw me down the stairs and turned the light off by the switch at the top of the narrow staircase. I could do nothing now other than stare into the darkness and wait to see what punishment would be meted out. George was older than me, I know, but he wasn't very bright – and anyway he hadn't lit the newspaper. He would probably get off with a verbal scolding. And so would Trevor.

It was my fault. There was no getting away from it.

I sat down on the damp floor opposite the coal chute, beside a large, very black pile of coal. A strange multiplicity of sensations seized me. I could not see, but I could feel, smell and hear more keenly than ever. I was in that part of the cellar that was below the office, and in a while I heard Auntie Blodwen and Auntie Agnes go in and slam the door shut. I could hear them talking above me.

'We're going to have to do something about that boy's behaviour,' Auntie Blodwen began. I knew she was referring to me.

'I can't believe,' Auntie Agnes said, 'that he would go into Linda's field and try to murder the horses.'

I thought that was a bit rich and I felt like shouting up at them through the floorboards and putting the record straight.

'He's capable of anything,' Auntie Blodwen said.

'He obviously doesn't like animals,' Auntie Agnes retorted. 'We'll have to keep an eye on the dog from now on.'

'And the cats and the rabbit,' Auntie Blodwen added, 'until we find a way of dealing with the boy once and for all. He doesn't respond to punishment like a normal child.'

'You'll have to think of something special.'

'Don't worry, I'll put my mind to it. I'll think of something.'

'I know you will,' Auntie Agnes said. And then they were quiet, and I knew that Auntie Blodwen was kissing Auntie Agnes. You can't live in the same house as somebody without knowing what they get up to.

The next time I went out to play I found myself on my own. I didn't mind. It suited me fine. I went to Knighton Woods, where the diversions were many and the forest a playground. Badgers and wild pigs were there to be seen when I stood still in one place for long enough. Hedgehogs and rabbits were more common friends, trusted playmates that you could get close to. Toads, frogs and frog-spawn were the playthings, and the mass of multi-coloured flowers, and trees whose foliage was every shade of green, yellow, white and brown, was the arena. Time was under my thumb. What I did not see one day I easily spotted the next.

I withdrew into myself, preferring my own company and that of animals rather than having people and other children around me.

There were five ponds in Knighton Woods, end-products from a stick of misplaced German bombs, and they retained my interest day after day. The water held beneath its surface a thousand forms of life that begged inspection; in winter it froze solid and I fearlessly skated across bridges of ice to island sanctuaries.

The River Roding, full of fish and toy boats, wound its lazy way through the trees, and at the end of the day the sun held on to the last minute before disappearing in a blazing amen, to leave the air full of summery sounds and smells. The insects persisted awhile then crawled under stones as I hopped, skipped and jumped over them in my rush to get back to the orphanage so as not to get into trouble for being late.

I remember the occasion when, alas, I was abominably late. Auntie Blodwen locked me in the cellar the minute I got back.

With quick movements, she took hold of me by the collar the moment I crept in through the side door. Propelling me through the kitchen, she opened the cellar door with her free hand and threw me headlong down the narrow, wooden staircase.

I don't know how long exactly she kept me locked in the cellar, but it was too long, longer than I had ever been locked down there before. I sat on the floor and listened through the floorboards while everybody had dinner in the dining-room. I moved to another part of the cellar and listened as the washing-up was done in the kitchen, and I listened under the office floor as those who wanted to, watched television. Realising they were not about to let me out, I climbed to the top of the coal-pile and, with difficulty, pushed the lid of the chute open. I expected light to pour in through the hole, but it was already dark outside. Time had flown. All I was rewarded with was an extra draught of cold air. I slid down off the coal-pile, crept up the stairs, and turned the light on with the switch at the top. I knew Auntie Blodwen would be furious, but I couldn't help it, I was so afraid. I moved to another part of the cellar and listened under the playroom floor as the other children played, and gradually in ones and twos were sent off to bed.

So this is my punishment for setting light to the stables, I thought to myself, they're going to keep me down here all night.

I sat down and thought of the prophet Jeremiah. Auntie Blodwen had not long before told us the story about him being thrown down a well by the king's officers. The floor of a well was not so different from the floor of a cellar, I supposed; muddy instead of damp and dusty. That's where she gets her wicked ideas from, I thought, the Bible. I'll end up nailed to a cross one day.

The house was quiet once the other children had gone to bed, and through the half-open coal-chute I heard the familiar, distant sound of a train as it pulled into the Underground station at the bottom of the hill. My thoughts turned to West Ham Underground station and those times, shivering on a cold platform or jumping off the wall outside to amuse myself and keep warm, I had waited till the early hours for my mother to return home from the pub.

Having the light on in the cellar was a mixed blessing. Although it made me feel safer in a way, it meant I was aware of the spiders that, appearing from nowhere, would race at a tempo from ceiling to floor or from one room of the cellar to another as if their life depended upon it. They needn't have worried, I wasn't going anywhere near them. I was getting out of there. I knew I was strong enough to pull myself up to the level of the open chute and small enough to climb through the hole and out into the front garden, but what to do then? I would cross that garden when I came to it, but I just knew I couldn't stay put in the cellar all night not knowing what was going to happen to me.

Suddenly the cellar door opened and, looking up, I saw Auntie Blodwen standing at the top of the stairs with Auntie Agnes behind her, looking over her shoulder.

'Who gave you permission to put the light on?' Auntie Blodwen called down to me in a threatening tone.

'I was frightened,' I called up to her.

As they came down the stairs towards me I noticed the hairbrush gripped tightly in Auntie Blodwen's hand, her knuckles red and white with tension. I'd missed my chance to escape through the chute. It was too late. Or was it? Standing up quickly, I tried to climb to the top of the coal-pile, but the chunks of coal, both big and small, gave way beneath my feet. By the time I reached the summit and had my head and a shoulder through the chute, Auntie Blodwen and Auntie Agnes both had a firm grip on my legs and they were pulling me back down. I held on tight to the rim of the chute with only my head sticking out and I refused to let go.

Then I heard footsteps on the pavement. Two people were walking briskly up the hill from the station. As they passed the orphanage I could see the tops of their heads above the privet hedge and I could hear them talking. They were in a world of their own; walking home after a night out, I dare say. They seemed so normal. I didn't know whether to cry out to them or not. Typical childlike inhibition gripped me. They were adults. Why bother? But, I was thinking quickly, what have I to lose?

'Oi! Hey!' I shouted in desperation, through the darkness.

They stopped and peered over the privet hedge towards the house and its front door. They were close enough to me, but my head was sticking out of the coal-chute at ground level and they couldn't see me.

'Heeey! Oi!' I called out to them. I must have sounded like a donkey braying.

It was surreal, my head being tickled by grass and narcissus hybrids. I looked out over the tops of the flowerbeds towards the privet hedge. The taste of hyacinth was on my lips, unknown fragrances in my hair, and my face was caked with a thick mascara of coal dust and tears.

Beneath me was the pit and two monsters had hold of my legs. They suddenly tightened their grip and dug their fingernails into my calves. It hurt so much I swore down at them.

'You fuckers.'

The couple on the pavement must have thought somebody was swearing at *them*. They quickly moved off into the shadows and continued their journey up the hill. If they were local people they would have known Gibblings Shaw was an orphanage and I suppose they would have half-expected to be abused by its residents.

I continued to hold on tightly to the rim of the chute with both hands, but Auntie Blodwen was beating me on the backs of the legs now with the hairbrush and punching me in the stomach with a clenched fist.

I gritted my teeth, determined not to loosen my grip, but eventually I let go with one hand to protect myself and the battle was lost. Omitting a loud *Fuuuuuuuuuuuuuuuuuck!* I was pulled through the chute and down on to the coal-pile. Auntie Agnes quickly grabbed hold of me and held me there as Auntie Blodwen undid my short trousers and pulled them down.

'No,' I screamed. 'Leave me alone. I'm sorry I was late. I'm sorry about the fire at the stables.'

Auntie Blodwen's hands and arms were black with dust and this made her particularly cross because I remember she had a strong aversion to dust and germs, especially coal dust and children's germs.

'You're not nearly as sorry as I am,' she said, as she began to beat me with the brush. There was something especially detestable about the heavy, wooden hairbrush with its large, flat, stinging surface.

'How dare you open the lid of the coal-chute?'

Whack.

'You filthy little guttersnipe.'

Whack.

'Thinking of running away, are we?'

Whack.

'And where do you think you'll run to?'

Whack.

'Back to West Ham, that hole you crawled out of?'

Whack. Whack. Whack.

In the coming weeks and months I was further humiliated in one way or another by Auntie Blodwen. She came down on me hard after the fire at the stables. The beatings were usually around the head or on the back of the legs, the arms or bare bottom. Auntie Agnes would hold me down in the office, the cloakroom, or in the cellar, while Auntie Blodwen laid into me. If any marks or bruises were noticeable afterwards, they didn't have to be explained away because Auntie Blodwen was allowed to hit us. I think it was legal.

The effect of this strict discipline began to manifest itself once more in angry outbursts, excessive guilty feelings, sleep disturbances, and other psycho-neurotic and psycho-physiological disorders such as bedwetting and headaches. Some marks and blemishes were visible, but they blended themselves in with the other cuts and bruises that, as a disturbed child, I naturally accrued fighting in the school playground, running amok in Lady Linda's field or falling out of trees in Knighton Woods.

Once, when Mr Thomas *did* ask me about a particularly nasty bump on my head, I explained it away with a made-up story about falling out of a tree while scrumping apples. I wouldn't have dared say anything against Auntie Blodwen at the time for fear of further retribution. Mr Thomas looked out of the open classroom window towards the woods that backed on to the playground and had no reason to doubt my story.

My education, at school and in church, continued apace. I was paraded to God's house four times a week and the latest gripe from the men in robes was that Premium Bonds debased the community's spiritual economy and were no more than an incitement to gamble. I wonder what those churchmen would have thought about today's National Lottery!

9

Middle-class Values

I soon began receiving visits at weekends from a *special* auntie and uncle. This auntie and uncle were special indeed because they came to visit me in particular. They weren't interested in any of the other children at the home, only me. I didn't know them from Adam and Eve, but I felt chosen and warmed to them, accepting that my luck had changed for the better and soaking up the kindness. They were so kind and patient with me and they always brought me presents. I was even allowed to sit in the office alone with this couple, which made me feel very important for once. I remember how unflappable they were and uncomplaining, ready to listen and calmly give me their attention and affection.

'My name is Diana and this is Richard,' she said to me, the first time we met. 'What's your name?'

I told them.

'We know. Auntie Blodwen told us,' Richard said, handing me a present, gift wrapped.

I went ahead and opened my gift, a *Rupert* manual (I called it my *Rupert* 'manual', so used was I to being told I was good with my hands – in other words, so used was I to being told that I would *only* be good for manual work when I left school). I've never forgotten its glossy cover and comforting smell. That's all I wanted to do at first, smell it and feel it. Then I opened its cover and discovered the family Ursidae, with thick, chequered fur.

'Is the manual really for me?' I asked.

'Yes, it's yours.'

I felt its smooth cover again and with my 'manual' still in my hands, I imitated my stepfather's facial expression, closing my left eye without screwing up my face. Then I began hopping around the office on one leg. My hops were long, economical and rhythmic.

'We have a boy the same age as you. His name is Dylan and he goes to school in Southend. That's where we live, by the sea. Have you ever been to the seaside?'

I couldn't understand why I had been singled out in this way for special treatment. *Rupert* manuals! The seaside! Where would it all end?

I learned in due course that they were prospective foster parents and I was soon to go and stay with them for a weekend to see how we managed together under the same roof. I don't know if it was meant eventually to be a long- or short-term fostering arrangement or if it was even leading up to adoption, but either way they couldn't have known what they were letting themselves in for.

After one of their visits to see me at Gibblings Shaw they helped me pack a bag. I took so much pride in showing them my dormitory. Auntie Maxwell always did her best to keep it clean and tidy, but nobody had ever taken the slightest interest before now. 'This is where I sleep,' I said, lifting the bag on to my bed.

'Where are your spare clothes?' Diana asked.

'Spare clothes? I ain't got no spare clothes.'

'Don't you have a change of vest and underpants?'

I pointed to the huge chest of drawers. 'Second from the bottom.'

We packed some items into the bag and returned downstairs with the overnighter practically empty.

Auntie Blodwen came out of the office to see us off. 'He can be a very good boy when he makes up his mind to behave himself,' she said, in a voice reserved for prospective foster parents. 'Now,' she said to me, 'do you think it would be a good idea to go to the toilet before you leave?'

I went along the corridor to the cloakroom toilet and Auntie Blodwen followed me in and closed the door. 'Well, get on with it,' she said. 'We haven't all day.'

I undid my flies and stood there, urging myself to *go*.

'You have a very long journey. You can't ask Uncle Richard to stop the car every five minutes because you've suddenly decided you want to spend a penny.'

Eventually I succeeded. I did up my flies and washed my hands with soap and hot water in one of the many sinks in the cloakroom.

Auntie Blodwen was now standing behind me and I could see her reflection in the mirror. She admonished me again. 'For heaven's sake, will you get a move on? I think he's ready now, Mr Davies,' she called to Richard as we returned along the corridor. 'Are you sure you won't have some lunch with us before you go?'

'No, really. Thank you, Miss Jones. We'd better make a start. It's Saturday and I expect the roads will be busy. We can stop along the way for a cup of tea and something if needs be.'

'Well, if you're quite sure.'

Richard's and Diana's car was parked outside, and they took me home in it with them. On the way they asked me how I was getting on at school. I didn't tell them I was bottom of the class, but I think they knew.

We turned left at Gants Hill and, gathering speed, made our way along the Eastern Avenue towards the Southend Road.

While his parents were fetching me, Dylan was being looked after by an uncle, a real one. As we arrived, they came together to the front door of the terraced house in Southend and let us into a small, brightly decorated hall.

'Let me take your bag,' the real uncle said to me.

I handed it over somewhat unwillingly.

'This is Terry,' Diana said, taking off my coat. 'And this is Dylan, and his Uncle Graham. Aren't you going to say hello, Dylan?'

Dylan was a little taller than me, beefier if I remember, and he was dressed in the same grey uniform clothes of the day as I was. His hair was longer and darker than mine and his 'hello' a little too 'Jack Philips-y' for my liking.

'Take Terry into the garden, then, and you can get to know one another,' Diana said to Dylan. 'Show him your tent. I'll make some tea for us all.'

Dylan showed me his tent which was erected in the back garden. I went in to have a look at the interior, and when I came out again Dylan had disappeared into the house.

While he was gone, I took a house brick that was handy and repeatedly threw it at the wooden supports of the tent. As the tent collapsed I took the supports one by one, stood them at an angle against the garden wall and, with my foot, started breaking them in two. By the time anybody realised what was happening it was too late. Every single upright and crossbar was broken.

'Mum, Dad. Stop him!' Dylan screamed, as he came into the garden again.

His parents and his uncle came rushing into the garden behind him.

Dylan's uncle, in whose mouth one would previously have thought butter would not melt, was suddenly extremely angry. 'Why,' he growled. 'You nasty little piece of work.' He grabbed me by the collar and violently pulled me away from the garden wall and the pile of broken sticks beneath it. Dylan was clinging to his mother, and his father was standing wide-eyed and speechless, distraught and staggered beyond belief.

I honestly didn't think I had done anything wrong at the time. It may take a psychiatrist to work that one out, but that's how I remember it. I was just having a good time and thoroughly enjoyed watching that house brick slam into the wooden sticks. And I loved the sound of splintering wood. Music to my ears, it was almost as tuneful as splintering glass.

They took me into the house and tried to make the best of a bad situation. But there were other little things that went wrong that day. When Dylan stopped crying over his tent, I made him cry over something else – as if unconsciously I deliberately wanted to upset him. I can't remember what it was, an indiscretion that I have deliberately eradicated from my conscious memory.

There were communication problems, too. When I wanted to go to the toilet I said I wanted to go 'Aa Aa's' and nobody had any idea what I was talking about until it was too late.

That evening they tentatively put me to bed in Dylan's room and, as the father read us a story, I made a rude noise. Making rude noises in front of prospective foster parents and their children is not the same as making rude noises in front of your biological family. It was a moment of introspection for all of us.

The next morning, after a phone call, Richard, the prospective foster father, drove me back to the children's home, dropped a florin into the top pocket of my school blazer, and left me at the front door with Auntie Blodwen in time to go to church.

She walked up the hill behind me and the other Gibblings and I could almost feel her cold stare on my back. On arrival, she pushed me into a pew in front of the other children and told me to get down on my knees and pray for forgiveness. When my eyes were closed she stuck two fingers in the top pocket of my blazer and deftly removed the florin. I never saw it, or Richard and Diana, again – ever.

The new school term began and after tea I would sometimes sit down and attempt homework at the kitchen table, the most peaceful corner of the house once the washing-up was done. But trying to do homework was futile. I didn't have a clue about any of it and there was nobody to explain things to me.

I was more successful with practical experiments. I remember Trevor helping me to stir some salt into a saucer of water and, after getting permission from Auntie Agnes, we left it in front of the electric fire in the office. We then went off to change the straw in the rabbit hutch.

When we returned to the office later, the water had evaporated, but the salt remained! We sat down at the kitchen table and wrote up our findings in the form of a poem, which I've forgotten, but I know that it began:

> Like salt dissolved in water we want to be
> lost and found . . .

Trevor's education, because he was dark-skinned and his parents were from India, was more complex than my own. Central government policy was that children should receive a Christian education. No thought was given to the assimilation, never mind integration, of ethnic minorities. Pluralism did not rule; it was not even facilitated. Christianity was studied in depth. The United Kingdom, with its long Christian tradition, wished to remain a kingdom united in Christianity, at least in name. Trevor, with his knowledge and understanding from a different Hindu background, felt compelled sometimes to compete with my alien culture rather than to communicate and get along in it.

Cultural diversity and equality of opportunity were seen to be negative things by the Establishment. Trevor's background wasn't recognised. Hindu festivals were not celebrated. The Aranyakas and Bhagavad Gita were unheard of, and therefore unread, and children and adults at the home, and the children and teachers at school responded to Trevor in less meaningful terms than was desired of us by him. Teachers generalised superficially when talking to him and their speech was stereotyped since they knew so little about him. He was a misfit on two accounts: his orphan status and his colour. Those who kept him at arm's length thought they had a plurality of good reasons for doing so.

As for me, I was brain-dead. I was being fed, clothed and sent to church. The LCC were enjoying their rights and privileges, and one day they would hand me back, be pleased with my awareness of middle-class values and moral code, and I would be sent to work in a factory with unpleasant workmates who abused themselves and those around them. An awareness of so-called middle-class values would not be enough to save me from them. I would join their ranks. The do-'God-ers' would leave me to flounder on the rocks of a factory floor while their own children prepared for university and beyond. There was never any prospect of me earning any qualifications to help me get a decent job when I left school.

One day Trevor and I found George dancing a Strauss waltz in the playroom with an imaginary partner and only his voice for accompaniment. We led him out of there and, collecting Barry and Andrew on the way, we went upstairs to play the gramophone, our homework abandoned.

We took the cumbersome machine from the cupboard on the

first landing and carried it into the dormitory. The collection of seventy-eight-revolutions-per-minute records was equally cumbersome and heavy. I wound up the gramophone, selected *The Poor People of Paris* from the pile of records, and placed it on the turntable.

As the music played, I mimicked playing the piano. I suppose I was going through the motions of being happy on the outside, but inside I was really sad because I didn't understand my homework. And I was deeply afraid of Auntie Blodwen's megaphone voice. It was always with me. I could not relax until I went to bed.

Across the landing, Pop had no choice but to listen through the closed sick-room door to Winifred Atwell's recording. Looking back, I bet his face must have almost twisted around the keys of his typewriter. The music was too heavy for Pop. He was full of Hallé Promenade Concerts and Viennese light music, preferably conducted by Sir John Barbirolli. Like *The Poor People of Paris*, Viennese light music was party music. But there were *parties*, and there were *parties*.

'Strauss,' I thought I heard Pop say, as he came out of the sick-room. 'Gaiety needs to be controlled.'

We removed Winifred Atwell from the turntable, took the clockwork train set out of its boxes under the beds, and spread it all over the floor. George was discouraged from getting too close because he was clumsy with his feet and would knock bridges over, demolish tunnels, and destroy whole stations with thoughtless steps. Ricky came into the bedroom and we allowed him to join in. There was a price exacted for the privilege: but he was happy to pay back the debt of gratitude with postage stamps. He went away and found his stamp album and then gave two stamps to each of us and sat down beside the track to watch the train go round and round.

Lady Barbirolli came to visit us soon afterwards. It was Pop's idea. He was well-acquainted with Sir John, who had taken over the Hallé Orchestra. We had tea in the dining-room and we talked. Lady Barbirolli seemed to understand her husband's subject even if we didn't.

'Conducting at the performance is the least important part of the business of conducting an orchestra,' she said. 'What counts most is the hard graft of marking and editing scores beforehand. Giving the true tempo to the orchestra is fundamental, of course. My husband always advises his students that no tempo should be so slow as to make it difficult for a melody to be *recognisable*, and no tempo so fast as to make a melody *unrecognisable*. But, more importantly, pass the bread and butter, please.'

She was down to earth, and The Buildings and the rub-a-dub-dub were a million miles away as she studied the plate of bread for a good few seconds as if reading a score, contrasting one slice against another before choosing white. We were always taught to take the slice that was nearest to us regardless of colour, and Lady Barbirolli's bad manners endeared her to us.

Looking around as she ate, she engaged us in conversation and seemed to show genuine interest in our concerns and in our health. There was for once a family atmosphere in the dining-room, perhaps revealing part of the art of being married to a famous conductor.

After tea we filed across the hall to the office and she took her oboe from its case and played for us. I directed her from my crouched position on the floor. With an unnatural gift of gesture, I conducted with a kind of youthful grandeur, trying to draw out the inward drama from Lady Barbirolli's notes; here with eloquence, there with vitality, and everywhere misinterpreting as well as not keeping time. The mini-concert was highly successful, music made righteous by my arm-flapping. There was a standing ovation and everybody laughed except Auntie Blodwen. As I had made myself known, Lady Barbirolli asked me if I liked music and I said that I did.

Her visit was like a breath of fresh air in the suffocation of my childhood; unassuming and genuine, she was the complete opposite to a 'do-God-er'. There was no patronage or superiority, she didn't single out any of us for flattery or prayers, but through her music she shared a kind of morality with us. Lady Barbirolli (Auntie Evelyn) won the battle that the priest and the Sunday school teacher had lost.

Auntie Maxwell, the cleaner, also took a particular interest in me and soon wondered if, along with another boy, I would like to go to her house every other Saturday to learn carpentry with her husband. Surprisingly, Auntie Blodwen gave her approval, saying that I was good with my hands and it would prepare me for possible work as a carpenter when I left school.

'If carpentry was good enough for Jesus,' Auntie Blodwen said to me, 'it's certainly good enough for the likes of you.' These were the days when if you worked with your hands you were thought less of than a person who had some kind of *office*, or someone who didn't work at all.

Auntie Blodwen had a point, though I'm loath to say anything complimentary about her. Jesus was rejected in his home town, partly because he was a carpenter, a working man. Nothing had changed. Prejudice and discrimination still ruled.

It was a short bus ride to Auntie Maxwell's on a single-decker which Trevor and I boarded outside the Underground station. Every seat on the red bus would be occupied with Saturday-afternoon shoppers. We would stand in the gangway, hold on to the hand rail, and fight back a feeling of disorientation as the bus sped through the streets. The more experienced shoppers were on their feet before the driver could shout

'Roding Road', pushing their way along to the exit at the front of the bus. Trevor and I were always glad to add to the crush, with wicked smiles on our faces as we forced our way along the length of the vehicle.

The house was halfway up a hill. We didn't even know it was a hill; we were so young, rough-and-ready.

Auntie Maxwell's husband made pianos in Harrods for a living and had a small workshop at the bottom of the garden that he used for his own pleasure at weekends. He would also restore furniture for friends and neighbours, if he thought it worth saving.

Before going down to the workshop, Trevor and I were given tea and chocolate biscuits which we took advantage of, emptying the tin as we watched Independent Television in the Maxwells' front room. There we remained, not wanting to be troubled with carpentry.

Eventually we were obliged to make our way along to the end of the garden, and Uncle Maxwell would help us to make something in wood: a small bookcase, a tool-box, a trolley, or whatever we had a mind to make. Trevor and I learned carpentry together for a while, but when Trevor dropped out, that was the beginning of the end for me, too. I wasn't really interested, and my indifference caused Uncle Maxwell to become impatient with me sometimes.

But it was expected that we would do something vocational rather than academic when we left school. So forceful was Auntie Blodwen in impressing upon me that I was going to be a carpenter, I actually began to believe it myself and started to collect tools. But nothing could have been further from the truth. I didn't want to be anything when I left school and I'd hardly given a moment's thought to growing up. My future was muddled by my past and I was still hoping for a childhood.

10

The Recreation Grounds

There was more fun to be had in the sandpit and on the swings and roundabouts than in an old man's workshop. I know Uncle Maxwell meant well, but I needed to 'get real'. The recreation grounds were surrounded by open fields that nobody seemed to mind us entering, and this was an added bonus if we wanted to let off steam and just rush around like mad animals.

We were allowed to play there unsupervised after tea sometimes and always instructed to behave ourselves and to be careful, especially with the younger children.

I was nine years old and careless and, without warning, was one day hit on the head as I ran in front of a swing. Patricia was standing on it and the edge of the wooden seat slammed into me at what felt like a hundred miles an hour.

I was knocked to the ground and there was blood everywhere as, dazed, I got to my knees and began to sob quietly.

'Terry,' screamed Patricia. She jumped from the swing and came over, helping me to my feet. 'You'll be all right, Terry,' she said. 'Don't mention this to anybody.'

I was gripped with fear as I felt the wound. The cut was deeper than anything I had ever put my fingers into. Patricia decided there and then to walk me to the hospital. It was close by, and a visit to the hospital was certainly a safer option than returning to Gibblings Shaw already covered in blood.

We went to Out-patients and I was dealt with straight away and given at least two injections, I remember, and a number of stitches. Information about my parents was asked for by the nurses, and when Patricia told them I had none, they became confused, sat me down for twenty minutes, and then let me go.

Auntie Blodwen was in the scullery as we came through the side door. She looked miserable, but she didn't seem too surprised by the mummy-sized bandage that was wrapped around my head. She told me to wait in the playroom and then, leaving what she was doing, she led Patricia into the office by the scruff of the neck.

In the playroom I pressed my ear to the partition wall to listen to what was being said next door in the office. Auntie Blodwen began speaking to Patricia in a voice that was as nasty and as menacing as anything I had ever heard.

'Patricia. Or shall I call you Pat, like your common friends do? Close the door – quietly.'

Patricia closed the office door and said 'hello' to Auntie Agnes.

Up until this point in time, I hadn't realised that Auntie Agnes was in the office.

Then Auntie Blodwen inquired: 'What happened to Terry?'

Patricia was slow in answering.

'I'm talking to you, young lady. Haven't you got a tongue in your head? What happened to Terry?'

'It was an accident, Aunt. Honest it was.'

'It didn't look like an accident to me, I saw it happen. I cut through the recreation grounds with the dog this afternoon. And don't call me "Aunt", you little guttersnipe. If you hadn't been standing on the swing, it wouldn't have happened. I suppose you enjoy the boys looking up your skirt. Is that why you were standing on the swing instead of sitting on it properly?'

'No, Auntie Blodwen.'

I imagine Auntie Blodwen turned to face Auntie Agnes at this point because she added, 'She enjoys boys looking up her skirt, Agnes.'

After a pause, Auntie Blodwen continued: 'How old is Terry?'

'He's nine,' Patricia said.

'And how old are you?'

'Thirteen, Auntie Blodwen.'

'Go to bed,' Auntie Blodwen said, wearily. 'I don't want to see you again until tomorrow morning.' I heard the door open. 'And before you go upstairs, tell Terry I want to see him.'

I took my ear from the wall and exchanged a glance with Patricia as we passed one another in the hall.

I must have looked a sight for sore eyes as I went into the office. I closed the door and Auntie Blodwen walked round me without taking her eyes off me. I looked at Auntie Agnes, but she, after barely catching my eye, looked away at nothing.

'Take your hands out of your pockets,' Auntie Blodwen said.

I took them out.

'That's better,' she sounded almost put out by my compliance. 'It's time to get a few things straight around here,' she said. 'Do you know how much it costs to keep you here? I was just working it out.' She sat down in Pop's armchair and instructed me to sit on the settee facing her. 'There's your food to begin with, you eat like a horse. Then there's your clothes, your silly little school uniform with its pretty badge, there's the running of this place . . .'

Auntie Blodwen, with Auntie Agnes following her lead, swept the room with her eyes. 'All the little extras . . . If you add it all up, it must be a lot of money. What do you think of that, Terry?'

'Nothing.'

'Nothing . . .?' There was a look of displeasure on her face and a gap of a few seconds before she spoke again. 'What were you doing at the recreation grounds today?'

'Nothing.'

'Nothing? Is that all you can say? Nothing!'

After a pause I said: 'I don't know what I'm supposed to say.'

'Just tell the truth, Terry,' Auntie Agnes said.

'Truth! Truth!' exclaimed Auntie Blodwen. 'He doesn't know the meaning of the word.'

'Yes I do . . .'

'Shut up.'

'Don't tell me to shut up,' I said, offended at last.

Auntie Blodwen looked at me evenly. 'What did you say?' There was real dislike in her voice.

I had unnerved myself. I wondered if I should have told her not to tell me to shut up.

'You guttersnipe,' she said. 'Serves you right you've got that bump on your head; if you hadn't been trying to look up Patricia's skirt when she was on the swing, it wouldn't have happened.' This really puzzled me and I began to feel faint. She was beginning to sound scary. I forced my attention back to the gathering torrent of words. Her mouth twisted as she spoke, the room started to spin, and I experienced my nightmare sensation. ZZZZZZZ was in my ears and everything around me felt heavy.

I honestly can't remember what happened next. One minute I was in the office and the next I was lying in bed waiting for getting-up time. If anything did happen, I must have eradicated it from my memory like so many other things. With my eyes, I traced the carpentered lines of the dormitory as the walls and ceiling seemed to make pincer movements towards my aching and bandaged head.

* * *

I took the bus to school. We had religious education first period and science the second (a magical mix if ever there was one). During the science lesson I put my hand up to ask a question. 'Why can't we learn about poisons? That's science, innit?'

'Yes,' said Mr Thomas. 'But why do you want to learn about poisons, Denby? Are you thinking of committing suicide by any chance?'

During the afternoon my mind was everywhere except where it should have been. I stared out of the closed classroom window and tried silently to work out a way of poisoning Auntie Blodwen without getting caught. Mr Thomas, meanwhile, was intent on getting us to draw charts and polygons and Noddy guides to the human body; mathematics and human biology. He loved teaching and lived for it.

That evening in the playroom I pretended to read *The Children's Newspaper*. Everything possible was done to stay on the right side of Auntie Blodwen. Between the pages of the newspaper I had a comic hidden, but my mind was not on the comic.

I had something far more sinister to think about, and I was waiting impatiently for bedtime. I exchanged another knowing glance with Patricia as she came back into the playroom from the scullery. For a long time there'd been a bond of kinship between us. She knew about the comic instinctively.

Pia was sitting at the table coughing over her doll. She was a good friend, too. A number of other children were amusing themselves this way and that, and the Irish setter was sitting quietly on the floor, thin and pretty, watching us with a dog's anguished look. She was an elegant dog, racy and stylish, and at the same time sensitive. She lifted her long head and gracefully stretched her whole body from nose to tail. Her coat almost glinted as she moved her deep muzzle into the air and sniffed at something. Relaxing again, she yawned noisily and closed her hazel eyes. It was bedtime.

The younger children started going upstairs first, to use the toilets and bathrooms, and then the bigger children followed on after them. I took my turn, and after I had washed and cleaned my teeth I lay awake in bed scheming for I don't know how long. Eventually I was aware of Patricia kneeling by the side of my bed. 'You OK, Terry?' she whispered.

I propped myself up on one elbow. She must have noticed that I'd been crying.

'I saw you in the playroom this evening, reading *The Children's Newspaper*,' she said, trying to cheer me up. 'Was it interesting?'

'What are we going to do?' I said.

George, asleep in the bed opposite, turned over, muttering.

'Dunno what to do,' said Patricia, at length, having waited with the patience of a saint until George was settled once more and breathing evenly again.

'Couldn't we poison her?'

Patricia considered this, and then rejected the idea.

I wasn't to be discouraged though, and after Patricia had gone back to bed and I was quite sure that everybody in the house was fast asleep, I slipped out of bed and tiptoed downstairs. In the office I took an empty Quink bottle and a large paper-clip from one of the pigeon-holes and placed them in the pocket of my dressing-gown.

Jenny whimpered next door in the playroom, and through the partition wall I whispered for her to be quiet. It was only me. She must have known that. I went along the corridor to the back door of the house. It was now or never.

I went out the back door and down the concrete steps to the

boiler-room. Opening the small padlock with the paper-clip was a piece of cake. I left the open padlock dangling from the staple and entered.

Once inside, I pulled the door shut behind me and paused to look around by the light of the moon that was decanting through the small window. The boiler was resting, but from earlier blasts the room was still warmer than any room I'd ever broken into and a thick smell of something strange hung around in the air. 'Right,' I thought to myself. 'Where's the weed-killer?'

I found the can and poured some of the liquid into the Quink bottle. Most of it went on the floor and was soaked up by the porous concrete, leaving an even stranger smell in the air. As an afterthought, before leaving I reached up and rifled the pockets of the gardener's overalls, which were hanging from a hook on the wall, and I was rewarded with a number of copper coins and a threepenny-bit. The threepenny-bit was old and grimy; a barely visible plant on one side that I thought was a wild thistle and the disciplined face of a monarch on the other. Unlike His Majesty King George VI, my face shone with excitement. I fondled the twelve-sided bit between thumb and finger before placing it in my pocket with the other coins and the Quink bottle. I went outside, pushed the boiler-room door closed again and, after replacing the padlock and doing it up, went back into the house.

Once back inside, I went to the cloakroom and put the weed-killer and money into the pocket of my school blazer that was hanging there on a hook, with two dozen other coats. Then I went back to bed.

In the morning before leaving for school I sneaked into the larder with my coat on, opened the door of the fridge and, taking the Quink bottle from my pocket, poured the weed-killer over the remains of a chicken that I knew had been put aside for Auntie Blodwen to finish.

Some of the weed-killer had leaked during the night. The material inside the pocket of my coat had been destroyed and I pondered what the liquid might do to the inside of Auntie Blodwen's belly.

I left for school on my own, but soon became aware of Patricia and Barry running after me.

'Terry, Terry,' they shouted.

When they were level with me, Patricia said breathlessly: 'Terry, Barry and me are not going to school today, we're going to Folkestone.'

'That'll be nice,' I said. 'Who with?'

'You,' Patricia said. 'Come on. We're running away. We've decided to let you come.'

11

Running Away

We backtracked through the side streets towards the Underground station. By the time we arrived there, it was fifteen minutes to nine. There was still time to change our minds and go to school. But Patricia seemed adamant, no turning back. Barry bought tickets and we went on to the platform and boarded a train, hearts thumping inside our little chests.

'We've done it,' I said to myself, as the automatic doors closed behind me. No turning back now. My courage surprised me.

'I put weed-killer on that chicken in the refrigerator,' I said to Patricia, as we sat down.

'Why?' she asked.

'To poison Auntie Blodwen.'

'But what about Auntie Agnes and Auntie Gladys and the other children? Do you want to poison everybody?'

'It's Auntie Blodwen's chicken,' I said. 'She's been saving it. And anyway Auntie Agnes is vegetarian.'

Patricia sighed and started to outline her plan to me. She had some money and distant cousins in Folkestone. We would make our way to Folkestone through the Blackwall Tunnel and stay with Patricia's relatives, at least to begin with.

We alighted at Mile End and started walking towards the Blackwall Tunnel. I thought we would never get there. On and on we went along the seemingly endless Burdett Road. I'd had my fair share of walking the streets of London before I was taken into care, but this was ridiculous. Nevertheless, we kept walking and eventually arrived at the tunnel entrance.

There were lights along the roof as we entered, and these disappeared around each new bend; the atmosphere was foreboding. The lighting seemed inadequate. We went deeper in, downhill thankfully, because we were so tired. Patricia was leading the way along the raised pedestrian walkway and Barry was sliding his hand along the handrail behind her as I brought up the rear.

The tunnel twisted and turned its way under the Thames and the traffic flowed constantly. The din was astounding, great echoes of sound. Barry was the first to complain.

'Can't we turn back? My ears, they're killing me.' He stopped walking and, with his hands over his ears, leaned against the handrail. The next car came round the bend and enveloped him in a cloud of exhaust fumes.

Patricia turned with her eyes closed, coughing: 'No. Keep going.'

Eventually, turning another bend, we saw some light in the distance. We quickened our pace. and the last hundred yards we ran uphill laughing and cheering. Barry forgot about his aching ears. We were on the outskirts of Greenwich, hungry and thirsty, and looking for a sign to Folkestone. To our dismay, there wasn't one.

As we walked on towards Greenwich we passed an enormous articulated lorry parked in a lay-by, and we ran round to the driver's side to ask for directions. Standing akimbo in the road, I called up to the driver: 'Oi! Is this the way to Folkestone, mate?'

He hesitated for a long while, looking down at us, and then said, 'Get in then.'

Before he could change his mind, we ran round to the nearside of the cab and clambered in next to him. The smell of the cab reminded me of the boiler-room at the children's home.

Pulling away into the stream of traffic, he produced a packet of sandwiches and shared them with us. We were absolutely famished and devoured them one after the other.

As we drove on, I noticed after a few miles that the driver, without speaking, kept looking across at Patricia and I started to feel uneasy. He was looking her up and down and studying her legs where her skirt had risen up over her knees. It didn't seem right to me, somehow.

Although Patricia was older than me, I suddenly felt deeply protective towards her in a way that nobody had ever felt about me and I wanted to get her out of there. It was the same feeling that I had had for Angela when she was being ridiculed by the boys at school because she wasn't wearing any knickers. But we needed the ride in the lorry; it was such a relief after all that walking. I didn't know what to do and started to panic inside. Mercifully, as we approached some traffic lights which were changing to red, the driver said this was as far as he was going.

He pulled up at the red light. 'Having a day off school, then?'

'We're on holiday,' Patricia said, as we clambered out of the cab as fast as we could.

'Gertcha,' he shouted after us.

We still had no idea where we were and kept running straight ahead until we could run no further. We walked another mile or so and then we were stopped by a police motorcyclist. He had been roaring along, unnecessarily because he was going nowhere, when he picked out the three of us ahead of him on the opposite side of the road.

He slowed down a little. At the very least we were playing truant, he must have thought. We should have had our lunch and been back in school by now, he would have reasoned. Don't recognise that uniform, either, he might have soliloquised. But as he passed he seemed to have second thoughts and accelerated away from us, thinking perhaps that we were simply late and on our way back to school. Nevertheless, the three of us froze, our eyes turned towards him in alarm. The police motorcyclist must have noticed our reaction in his mirror because he slammed on his brakes and brought the bike to a screeching halt. He ran back along the pavement towards us, waved the traffic down, and crossed over to our side of the road. He walked smartly up to Patricia. She was obviously the eldest and was now standing on the kerb wide-eyed.

'Right,' the police motorcyclist said.

I took two steps backwards and must have looked about ready to do a runner.

'You stay where you are,' the policeman jeered at me. 'I need to know what's going on here.'

Nothing we had to say made any sense whatsoever, so he called up a car on his radio with a view to taking us in. Within no time at all the car came out of nowhere. It was a black Wolseley with a bell ringing at the front and two policemen inside.

The motorcyclist strode across to his partners as the bell was turned off and he explained to them more comprehensively than he had on the radio what was going on.

'Look,' I remember him saying, 'I'll stay with the girl. Would you do us a favour? Each of you takes a boy aside and sees what sort of story he gives?'

He went over to where Patricia was standing. 'Are you OK?' he asked. 'You look worn out. What's your name, love?'

'Anne,' she lied.

I couldn't hear what Barry was saying to his policeman, but he looked irritated – the policeman I mean. He was searching Barry and struggling to remove everything that a schoolboy carries in his pockets to Folkestone.

I gave the policeman who interrogated me an even harder

time. 'I don't have to tell you nothin', mister,' I said, when he asked me my name.

'I need to know your name and address,' he insisted.

There was silence. He stood there, frustrated. Then he leaned forward, put the fingers of his hand under my chin, and jolted my head upwards. I recoiled, and immediately looked down at the pavement again.

It was two days since I'd been hit by the swing and the bruise was coming out. The left side of my face was blue and the right side, although I was standing up to the policeman, was as white as the bandage that was still wound around my head.

'You are going to tell me your name and address,' the policeman said, in a high-pitched voice. 'I don't care if we have to stand here all day.'

My eyes blazed momentarily at him before I returned my gaze to the pavement.

'Let's try again,' he said.

'No,' I replied, still looking down. 'Fuck off.'

'Right, in the car,' he said. 'There's obviously no point in trying to be courteous with the likes of you.'

He manhandled me into the back of the Wolseley and I felt very much at home there. In a little while Patricia and Barry were put into the back of the car with me and we were driven off.

At the police station, the policeman who had interrogated Barry put a call through to the children's home and then it became obvious to Patricia and me that Barry had spilled the beans. Auntie Gladys answered the telephone and we heard her crepitant voice on the other end of the line.

'No, no . . . I can assure you they are not. Auntie Blodwen has gone to the hospital, that's all. What are their names? Oh! My aching back.'

While we had been eating sandwiches with the lorry driver, Pia had been on tiptoe in the dining-room at Gibblings Shaw peeping through the service hatch as Auntie Blodwen ate her lunch in the kitchen. Pia had been sent home from school having complained of feeling unwell, and had had nothing better to do than spy on people. Auntie Blodwen's lunch consisted of a chicken sandwich made from thick slices of white bread and tons of English mustard (as Pia had put it) which Auntie Blodwen had a craving for.

Of course, we couldn't have known any of this; it all came to light later when Pia gave us a full account of what happened at the home while we were in Greenwich.

As I say, Pia had been on tiptoe in the dining-room, watching and listening through the service hatch as Auntie Blodwen tucked into the sandwich. The dripping hot mustard took away the taste of the weed-killer and she was into her fifth bite before she thought it didn't taste as good as it ought to.

'Ugh,' she said, standing up. 'There's something wrong with this.' She leaned both palms on the table and claimed to be feeling ill.

Auntie Gladys brought her basin of vegetables from the kitchen sink to get a better look at her.

'Whatever's come over you?' she gasped, over her bowl. 'You look absolutely dreadful.'

Auntie Blodwen raised her hand to her mouth. And so did Auntie Gladys, because the kitchen was her domain. Food was her responsibility.

'I'll just go upstairs and lie down,' Auntie Blodwen said, clutching her throat.

'Shall I call the doctor?' asked Auntie Gladys.

It was five-past four when the doctor arrived and the children were already returning from school. Auntie Blodwen was in bed feeling much worse and she couldn't speak. Auntie Agnes, back from the shops, explained to the doctor that Auntie Blodwen had eaten some chicken that hadn't agreed with her.

'It's not that,' said the doctor, looking down at Auntie Blodwen. 'She's taken something toxic. The inside of her mouth is swollen and burned, her stomach too, I shouldn't wonder. She'll have to go to hospital.'

Auntie Gladys was holding her head in her hands outside the bedroom door.

'Has she tried to do anything like this before?' the doctor asked.

'What are you talking about?' said Auntie Agnes. 'She has not tried to do anything. You're not suggesting she's suicidal?'

'We haven't time to talk. Where's the telephone?'

'Downstairs.'

The ambulance arrived and the children gathered round, excited, as Auntie Blodwen was put in the back on a stretcher and Auntie Agnes and Betty, the senior girl, sat down beside her.

The doors were closed and the ambulance sped away with its blue light flashing.

Auntie Gladys was now alone in the front garden with the children and found herself having to shout, like a teacher who has lost control of her class. 'Andrew, will you *please* come inside? Jenny, leave Ricky alone. Go inside at once. Eddy, there's washing-up still to be done in the scullery. Ask Angela to dry. Ena Peters, come and help me in the kitchen.'

Word had already gone round among the children that we had run away, and they now closed ranks and took measures to cover our absence. Our places were unlaid in the dining-room and our chairs were placed against the wall and the remaining ones spaced out so that there were no gaps at the tables. When everybody sat down, it would now be much less evident that three children were missing.

It was half-past five when they sat down. If they had known at the Stratford office that the cook had been left in charge, they would have had a collective blue fit. Auntie Gladys had to be reminded to say grace, and then the children talked with their mouths full and threw food at one another. Auntie Gladys ate very little.

The children finished their tea and went into the playroom, and while Auntie Gladys was doing the washing-up the telephone rang in the office. It was the policeman from Greenwich on the line asking if any children were missing.

'No, no,' said Auntie Gladys.

'The thing is,' said the policeman, 'we've picked up some children and they claim to be yours.'

'I can assure you,' Auntie Gladys said, 'they are not. Auntie Blodwen has gone to the hospital, that's all. What are their names?'

'Their names are Barry, Patricia and Terry.'

'Oh! My aching back,' Auntie Gladys said.

That was Pia's story.

Betty, although she wasn't as articulate or as bright as Pia, was later able to give us a graphic account of what happened at the hospital. Betty had watched through an open door as Auntie Blodwen had a tube put down her gullet and the contents of her stomach were aspirated or 'sucked out' as Betty put it. The doctor, Betty reported, stooped down at the side of the bed and watched closely as the flask filled.

Auntie Blodwen proceeded to wet the bed, but the doctor was pleased about this because it indicated to him that her kidneys were functioning as they should. She was then given a bedpan and encouraged to open her bowels because the doctor wanted to see if there was any blood in her faeces. Being a trained nurse, Auntie Agnes zealously helped put the bedpan in place.

After the tube was removed from her gullet, Auntie Blodwen was given two tablets with a large glass of milk. Betty thought the nurse had called them active-charcoal tablets, but she wasn't sure.

The doctor then went and called the police on a telephone that was next to where Betty was standing. It was normal practice for the police to be informed about incidents of a suspicious nature and the doctor was suspicious. Suicide attempts had a certain hallmark to them and this patient's reactions to being saved lacked some of the usual characteristics.

By the look he gave Betty, the doctor was already thinking that the children at the home might have had something to do with it and he said as much on the telephone to the police, adding that he believed the poison was administered about three hours before the housemother was admitted – that is to say, lunchtime – and she was very lucky to be alive.

The doctor couldn't have known, but what happened to Auntie Blodwen was fitting treatment for somebody who was so disgusted by other people's illnesses.

Auntie Agnes and Betty returned to Gibblings Shaw and Auntie Gladys told them that we were in Greenwich and the police were bringing us back that evening. Auntie Agnes went into the office, folded her arms, and looked out of the window.

That was Betty's story.

We were returned to Gibblings Shaw in a police car and one of the policemen said to Auntie Agnes that a report of the incident would have to be made and, if any more information were needed, somebody would come over from Greenwich and she shouldn't be surprised if she received another phone call. As soon as the policemen had gone, the three of us were locked in the cellar, as punishment, but also for security.

Above our heads we could hear Auntie Gladys working overtime in the kitchen and imagined that her eyes must have been filled with a look of pain at the thought of what there was still left to do after all the distractions. She was preparing one or two things for breakfast with one hand, by the sound of it, and peeling potatoes with the other.

We knew our way around down there, and as we ventured under the playroom we could hear the dog snoring in her basket, huddled up near one of the huge cast-iron radiators. We went to the front of the cellar and Barry climbed to the top of the coal-pile and tried to push the round lid of the chute open an inch to let some light in. It wasn't easy. The lid was a tight fit and made of heavy metal. The harder Barry pushed, the more the coal gave way beneath his feet. Eventually he succeeded and, with a metal clank, a slither of light penetrated the darkness. We could have escaped through the chute, then and there, into the front garden. But what good would it have done us? Barry came down off the pile, coal-black, but smiling. And then, as I looked round, I could see not one, but two gigantic spiders on the wall in front of me. I just knew they were looking at me.

'Can you see what I can see?' I whispered to Patricia.

She had seen. And I knew what she was thinking. Like me, she was wondering what else was lurking unseen down there in the shadows.

Suddenly the telephone rang above us, and we went and stood beneath the office and listened to Auntie Agnes's side of the conversation through the cobwebbed floorboards above our heads.

'Hello . . . the police?' Auntie Agnes said, not knowing she was talking to an officer from our local police station who was calling about Auntie Blodwen's poisoning, but instead mistakenly thinking she was talking to Greenwich police station about us runaways.

'You'd like to talk to the children . . .? You think they're to blame . . .? Well, of course they're to blame. D'you think it's my fault? *Of course* the children are to blame, all three of them . . . Of course I know there were three of them. How could I not know? Don't *you* know? Don't they tell you anything at the police station . . .? When would you like to talk to them . . .? You'll be here in fifteen minutes . . .?'

Auntie Agnes replaced the telephone receiver. She knew police cars were fast, but she must have thought the policeman was being optimistic in thinking he could get to Woodford from Greenwich in fifteen minutes. Unless, she thought, they had already left Greenwich and were calling her on the car radio?

She reluctantly let us out of the cellar, and when the knock at the door came Auntie Agnes invited the policemen in and presented us to them in the hall. There were two of them. A plain-clothes man, with a uniformed bespectacled junior officer at his side. They removed their headgear.

'These are the ones,' Auntie Agnes said, nodding towards us.

I don't know why, perhaps the bandage on my head made me look conspicuous, but the policemen took a fancy to me and took me into the office before the others and sat me down. I imagine Auntie Agnes kept a close eye on Patricia and Barry outside in the hall.

I was immediately stereotyped by the policeman and his colleague as being young, illegitimate and from the East End. My type would inevitably exhibit unpleasant hostility and my status simply did not need further examination.

'How old are you?' he began.

'I'm nine,' I said.

'Why did you do it?'

'I don't like it here,' I replied, thinking I was being asked why I had run away. 'Auntie Blodwen gives me too much grief.'

'That's not a reason to try and kill her.'

I was taken aback. How could he know? I felt the blood drain from my bruises.

'You're a would-be murderer, Terry.'

I was thinking hard.

'I know that boys bent on violence rarely act on their own, so I want you to tell me who helped you. Was it Patricia and Barry?'

'Have you got any proof?' I said.

The policeman ignored my question, probably thinking that it was the height of impertinence.

'You're a coward, Terry. You need the support of others to bolster your actions. I want you to tell me what part Barry and Patricia played in all of this. I know that at lunchtime today you put something toxic in the housemother's dinner. What was it? And who helped you?'

I saw a way out.

'Come on, Terry. Don't insult my intelligence. I want to know. You came back from school at lunchtime and administered something to the housemother's dinner. What was it?'

'I didn't go to school today,' I said.

'So you were here all the time,' the policeman said, satisfied, feeling he'd made a breakthrough.

'No,' I said. 'I've been down in Kent all day. I can prove it. Barry and Patricia were with me, locked up in a police station. How could we poison Auntie Blodwen if we were that far away, and locked up?'

The junior officer removed his spectacles and began to clean the lenses with a handkerchief. At the same moment there was a knock on the door and Auntie Agnes came in to ask if either of the dicks wanted a cup of tea.

'Has this boy been to school today?' the plain-clothes policeman asked. He had a strange look on his face.

'Of course not,' Auntie Agnes said, 'How could he?'

'Has he been out today?'

'I should say so. He's been gallivanting around Greenwich since half-past eight this morning. You must know that?'

'But you said he was to blame?'

'And I meant it. He's nine years old and big enough to take responsibility for his own actions. Are you going to speak to the other two?'

'No,' said the policeman, putting his hat on. 'That won't be necessary.'

Auntie Blodwen was detained at the hospital for observation and an emergency auntie was sent to Gibblings Shaw for a day or two to help Auntie Agnes look after us. Her name was Auntie Maori and she was from New Zealand. We children at the home warmed to her because she was so kind and she seemed concerned about my bandaged head and wanted to know what had happened. There were no hugs or kisses, she didn't go that far, but we knew she had our best interests at heart because she would argue with Auntie Agnes, saying that she was too strict with us and she should keep her hands to herself. We were embarrassed when they rowed in front of us. Watching two grown-ups rowing, and even fighting (Auntie Maori was bigger than Auntie Agnes so she wasn't going to be intimidated), made us feel even more insecure, if that were possible; and although we really appreciated what Auntie Maori was trying to do, it didn't stop Auntie Agnes lashing out at us whenever she had a mind to and it just made our lives as traumatic as ever.

Auntie Maori went out of our lives as suddenly as she had entered, and Auntie Blodwen was allowed home from the hospital on the same day I went there to have the bandage removed from my head and have my stitches out. We walked back to Gibblings Shaw together. I felt so insignificant beside her, carrying her bag, trying to keep up as she paced impatiently up the hill with a horrible look on her face.

Inquiries about a suspected attempted murder were discontinued on the assumption that Auntie Blodwen had indeed tried to do herself in because we were all getting to be too much for her. She was advised to seek psychiatric help and there were no further repercussions. I was never going to win the war against Auntie Blodwen, but I'd won a battle and I felt good about that, for a while at least.

12

Riding My Bike

On Saturday afternoons those of us who were old enough were allowed to go out on our own, and those of us who had bikes were allowed to use them. We were even given a small amount of pocket money, a few old pence of taxpayers' money, but it was enough to buy some sweets or a few cigarettes. The shopkeepers were usually happy to sell cigarettes to us, but if they made a fuss we simply said, 'They're for my dad.'

I choked on the cigarettes, but also on those words 'They're for my dad'. If only I really had a dad to send me down to the shops on Saturday for cigarettes, I would have been so proud to have uttered those words and would have meant them.

I remember one Saturday afternoon, getting my bike out and, without telling anyone, cycling all the way to West Ham. I had to be quick. It was a long way to go and be back in time for tea to avoid the risk of being shouted at and beaten.

To get to West Ham I had to go through Snaresbrook and then over Wanstead Flats before reaching the East End. I had a milometer attached to the front wheel of my bike and I would keep one eye on that and the other on the road. I tried to keep an eye on the time as well.

On Wanstead Flats there was a large number of Nissen huts, and as they came into view I would ride off the road on to a track of brown earth and zigzag between them. The Flats were a large area of uncultivated common heathland on the outskirts of East London. Cattle were allowed to graze there legally and the animals often crossed over the main road and wandered through the town. Nobody could stop them because of the law that existed to protect their rights.

Every year a fair arrived and stalls and amusements were erected. When the fair packed up and left, model-aeroplane enthusiasts flew their machines all day till dusk.

In my day, clandestine lovers on motorbikes with side-cars used the Flats as somewhere to go. Apart from these infiltrators, there were the residents who lived in the Nissen huts.

I sang on my bike as I crossed the Flats on my way to West Ham, a strange repertoire of songs mixed into one: 'Hitler has only got one ball . . . Rule Britannia, two tanners make a bob, three make one and six and . . . We are some of the Gibblings . . . Three German officers crossed the line, parlez-vous?' With the rattling of the bicycle, they formed a nervous yet interesting medley.

When I reached West Ham and Manor Road Buildings I was always too scared to knock on the door of my mum's flat, afraid, especially, of rejection. I just cycled round and round the blocks of flats, claiming my inheritance that way, before returning, via the Flats, to the children's home in Woodford (Sir Winston Churchill's constituency).

There was the usual turnover of children at the home and one day I found myself sitting with Betty at the closed office window on a straight-backed chair waiting for Miss Abbott to come and fetch her. She was leaving. Suddenly she seemed to feel a sense of anti-climax. She was going home, but what to? She had seen her parents half a dozen times in as many years. Miss Abbott would drive her the few miles to London and then keep in touch, visiting regularly to see how she was making out.

We watched the vehicles pass up and down the steep hill, but none stopped. Betty sat there in her Sunday best, having dressed herself with more than usual care. She was still as thin as ever.

Her wiry NHS spectacles were perched right on the end of her nose where she found them to be most comfortable. Her eyes were large behind the lenses. Auntie Blodwen came into the office to collect some ornaments and spoke to her.

'All you have to look forward to until you are sixty is hard work. From now on you'll have to work for your keep. You're growing up, Betty. You'll soon be a woman. Your mother needs you . . .'

Betty looked disturbed. She suddenly stooped forward despondently, her elbows on her knees, her chin in her hands. I don't think she wanted to grow up at that particular moment; she didn't want to be a woman and to look after a mother she hardly knew. The prospect must have daunted her. I slipped out of the office before Auntie Blodwen had finished speaking.

Fifteen minutes passed before Betty was able to announce the arrival of Miss Abbott. Auntie Agnes came from the kitchen, drying her hands on a tea towel, and Patricia began to cry quietly in the hall.

Miss Abbott came through the front door as Auntie Agnes opened it. She caught sight of Patricia. 'My! What's up with you? You'll flood the cellar if you don't pack that in.'

Auntie Gladys came along the corridor, drying her hands on her apron. Auntie Blodwen was unconscionably upstairs and didn't come down for that last goodbye.

'Goodbye, Betty. Do try and be good. Write to us. Let us know how you are getting on.'

'Yes, Auntie Agnes. I'll be all right, don't worry.'

'Oh, I shan't worry.' These were Auntie Agnes's last words to Betty.

'Goodbye, Betty,' said Auntie Gladys.

Miss Abbott and Betty took their leave and the front door was closed before they reached the end of the gravel path. I watched through the closed window in the porch as Miss Abbott's car was set in motion and disappeared down the hill.

Patricia was wiping her eyes with a white, cotton handkerchief as Auntie Blodwen came down the stairs, sighing heavily: 'Has Betty gone?'

'Yes,' sniffed Patricia.

'I hope she will be all right. She's had a hard time one way and another. She seems such a baby to be sending off like this. If only her father had been around more to help.'

'They've all got to go sometime,' Auntie Gladys said. 'Don't worry, she'll grow up and change her feathers. And as for her father, I'm sure no father alive could do more than you for these children. You think of nothing else. You should take more care of yourself.'

'Close the back door, dear, will you?' Auntie Blodwen said. 'Somebody has left it open again.'

Auntie Gladys closed the door and hurried back to the kitchen sink.

Auntie Blodwen followed her, and at the kitchen table continued to dust the bric-à-brac she had brought from the office earlier. I secretly watched her through the service hatch as she lifted the pieces one by one from the kitchen table, mentioning to Auntie Gladys where and how they had been bought. Auntie Gladys paused at the sink to listen as Auntie Blodwen gave a running commentary.

It had always been obvious to me that Auntie Gladys was as afraid of Auntie Blodwen as I was. She was cowed by mismanagement and mismanaged by a cow. She did everything that Auntie Blodwen asked of her, at the double and with the pretence that nothing was too much trouble. I could easily see through it and I was also old enough to understand that the biggest problem for children who are being abused in care is that everyone is afraid to say anything in case they lose their job or their promotion is overlooked. Auntie Blodwen had been given a small amount of power by the LCC and she was making the most of it. And nobody was willing to stop her or even to tell her off. All we children could do was keep as far away from her as possible and avoid her at every opportunity, but living in the same house and being dependent upon her for basic needs, it wasn't easy.

By the beginning of the summer holiday Betty's place in the dining-room had been taken. Miss Abbott came through the front door with the new girl as Pop appeared at the top of the stairs on his way to the bathroom. He was obliged to change direction and come downstairs to say 'hello'. Vera was introduced to all of us present and Miss Abbott probably assumed Pop was simply paying a visit. He never came out of the sick-room without his shoes, waistcoat and the jacket of his suit on, so he hardly looked as though he had just got out of bed.

For me, another year of school life was over. The end-of-year ceremony was brief: an assembly in the main hall with a talking-to from the Headmaster.

I spent the summer quietly on my bike, riding round Lady Linda's field and through Knighton Woods. Occasionally I would ride down to the recreation grounds with another boy and play on the swings and roundabouts, but I preferred the shyness of the forest paths and the seclusion and unsociability of the open country. Sometimes I would cycle away from the town for miles, on my own, my pedalling becoming faster and faster. Perhaps I was searching for something, or maybe still running away.

Sir Anthony Eden resigned as Prime Minister on the grounds of ill health, but nobody was fooled; least of all we schoolchildren. The truth was that British troops had had to withdraw from Egypt and hand control of the Suez Canal to a United Nations force.

The snow melted, and winter turned to spring. I celebrated my tenth birthday.

The brighter weather and my double-figures age didn't mean I stopped watching television, even if the screen was a tiny 12″ and BBC was the only station available. On the contrary, I was becoming an addict of *Children's Hour* during the week and on Saturday I boarded the *Six-Five Special*, the new teen show hosted by Pete Murray and Josephine Douglas. I was only ten, but I couldn't wait to grow up.

Six-Five Special's resident band was Don Lang and his Frantic Five, and guests on the show included the mocking Wee Willie Harris and Tommy Steele, Britain's answer to Elvis. Still only one television channel and, whatever the quality of the picture, it was how it was meant to be. But I made the most of it, and for a while was able to escape into this other world of rock 'n' roll.

13

Giving Away My Sweets

It was a weekday and the office was full of children who had rushed back from school to watch *Children's Hour* on the television before having their tea.

If you sat on the settee you had a sideways-only view of the screen and your neck ached. If you sat on the floor, you got pins and needles.

I sat on the floor and we watched *Sooty* with Harry Corbett and *Crackerjack* with Eamon Andrews.

When the programmes ended Auntie Blodwen came and announced tea was ready. One day she was about to switch off the television when something caught her eye. It was a news clip of Elvis Presley performing on stage in Los Angeles. Perhaps she really was human after all, I thought, because she stood there and watched without taking her eyes off the screen or so much as blinking. At the same time she was gesturing with an outstretched arm for us children to leave. We stood up, cursing under our breath. We left Auntie Blodwen watching Elvis and crossed the hall to the dining-room.

What I saw now was even more improbable than Auntie Blodwen watching Elvis Presley on the television.

I stopped dead in my tracks. A ladder was standing at the bottom of the staircase, resting against the frame of the glass partition above the balustrade. Halfway up the ladder, bucket of water in one hand, chamois leather in the other, was Fishy. He happened to look down just then and his eyes met mine. I stared back and then he turned away and continued with his work. I'd never forgotten Fishy. I still thought of him as a father, much more than I thought of Joe as a father. It was not that Fishy had behaved paternally towards me – unless, that is, his quiet acceptance of me could be viewed as a kind of paternalism. Had he really come to clean the windows now or was he seeking me out?

Carole walked into the back of me and cursed loudly. 'Why don't you look where you're going?'

'Why don't you go where you're looking?' I replied, still looking up at Fishy. 'He's my dad.'

She couldn't help emitting a small, suppressed giggle as she walked round me into the dining-room. She could giggle unsolicitedly as much as she liked. I was in earnest.

Fishy continued to the very top of the ladder. I felt denied and all I understood in that moment was that away from the familiarity of the East End, Fishy was like a fish out of water.

In the dining-room my place was now at the Top table, in the bay of the window, away from the grown-ups. I sat down. Zsa Zsa and Ricky gave out the plates of food and everybody closed their eyes and put their hands together and we said grace.

'Do you like Elvis?' Barry said to Auntie Blodwen, as we reopened our eyes and started to eat.

She didn't bother to answer. She must have thought Barry's question impertinent.

'He's my dad,' I said.

'Who?' Auntie Blodwen asked. 'Elvis Presley?'

Everybody laughed uncontrollably, including Auntie Blodwen.

'No, the window-cleaner is my dad.'

This could have been the signal for even more laughter, but my words had come out too choked, even for a clown. There was silence suddenly and everybody turned to look at me. There were tears in my eyes. I had no reason to make up such a story. And then again I had every reason.

'What makes you think the window-cleaner is your father?' Auntie Agnes asked.

'I just know he is,' I said, 'that's all.'

'Don't be so feeble-minded,' Auntie Blodwen sneered. 'You do not have a father. You have a stepfather, Joe Smith or whatever his name is, the man your mother was wedded to recently. Isn't it bad enough that you're illegitimate without you finding it necessary to go around mentally climbing up ladders to find a father who may be dead anyway? Now stop crying, you silly, sniffling little idiot and eat your food. And remember, there are children in Africa and India who don't have any tea.'

After tea, the other children watched television and I followed Fishy around and watched him clean the windows with his chamois leather until Auntie Blodwen came along the corridor and asked him if he wanted a cuppa.

'Come into the kitchen,' she said, beckoning him to follow her.

I went back into the dining-room to listen through the service hatch to what was being said. Auntie Gladys was doing the washing-up.

Pop was reading the newspaper. ''Bout time too,' I heard him say, as he cuffed the paper with the back of his hand. 'The Church of England is going to allow divorcees to take Communion.'

'I thought marriage was for life,' Auntie Blodwen said. And then in the same breath she said to Fishy, 'Come in, come in, Mr?'

'Grant,' said Fishy, as he went into the kitchen.

'Your name is not Denby?'

'No.'

'Smith?'

'No. Why?' Fishy's hands, always used to having something in them, fidgeted nervously until Auntie Gladys came to his rescue with the cup of tea.

'That boy who was watching you just now thinks you are his father,' Auntie Blodwen said. 'Do you know the boy?'

Fishy put his hand to his mouth and coughed. 'I do know the boy, yes.'

'And are you his father?'

'No, I'm bloomin' well not. His mother used to be a client of mine, that's all. I used to clean her windows.'

'There you are, Terry,' Auntie Blodwen said loudly. She knew I was listening behind the service hatch. 'You are letting your imagination run away with you again. The window-cleaner is not your father.'

Fishy seemed relieved to hear this and he started to relax a little. There was some loose conversation and Fishy volunteered to Auntie Blodwen that my mother played the piano and worked as a pub musician.

'What sort of music does she play?' Pop asked, obviously interested.

'She can play anything,' Fishy said. 'Serioso.'

If Pop was a gentleman, his daughter Blodwen was no lady. She had gleaned the information she wanted and there was no need to detain Fishy any longer. And what's more, the window-cleaner, from a totally different social background, had found it possible to use an Italian musical term in her kitchen. What next? This had gone as far as it was going to go. She took Fishy's cup and saucer from him. 'If you've finished your tea, you'd better get back to work,' she said.

I ran into the garden and climbed to the top of the silver birch. The branches were damp and slippery, the leaves budding immaturely around me. Alone in my tree, I watched as Fishy came into the garden with his ladder to clean the outsides of the windows. He didn't even know I was there, observing him. So much for putting my hopes on him. I would have to look to some other place for a father or father-figure.

Parents and other interested parties were allowed to visit the children of Gibblings Shaw on the second Sunday of each month, and here too there were blighted hopes. Every month there were to be seen in the playroom the disappointed faces of children whose relatives had not turned up. I knew the feeling only too well, having so often sat on my own, waiting, hoping somebody would come. As the afternoon wore on I would go walkabout, giving away my sweets to other children and their visitors. I once gave away a whole box of Bassett's Liquorice Allsorts, some sherbet, two edible flying saucers, a gobstopper and half a packet of wine gums to try and break into a family circle. But I couldn't buy love with confectionery, and at the end of the visit I had neither one nor the other; no love and no sweets, and no status. Having a visitor somehow gave you status.

However, this particular Sunday my mother made the effort to visit me and she dragged my stepfather along with her on his crutches. It was soon after Fishy had cleaned the windows and it was the first and last time she visited Gibblings Shaw. I wondered even then if my mother wasn't still seeing Fishy, though she was now married to Joe, my stepfather. It felt as though after Fishy had cleaned the windows at the children's home, he had gone back to The Buildings and reminded my mother that she had an eighth child.

I've often wished I could have been a passenger on the train that brought my mother and Joe to Gibblings Shaw, listening to their certain apprehensions about the visit. From the dining-room window I watched as they stopped outside in the road, reaffirmed to each other that they were standing outside the right gate, and then plucked up the courage to open it.

They came along the path towards the front door. My stepfather was wearing a dark suit with the right trouser leg pinned up to the waistband, and my mother wore a long, white woollen coat. A coat like that, with its large collar and huge buttons, was all the fashion at the time.

Auntie Agnes opened the front door to them and, in a voice reserved for parents and devoid of pleasantry, asked: 'Is this your first visit?'

'Yerst.'

'Mr and Mrs . . .?'

'Smith.'

'Go through to the second door on the right. The boy is waiting for you.'

I was indeed waiting, with my ear to the door. I moved aside as the door opened.

My mother had some parcels with her and she gave them to me. The three of us then sat down on straight-backed chairs in a group. It was *our* group. I felt so much pleasure and relief that at last someone was there for me. I opened the parcels: a clockwork fireman, a plastic trumpet, and lots of sweets and chocolate. I was disappointed with the trumpet because, like my watering-can, it was more like a toy than the real thing.

More visitors arrived and came iffily into the playroom. And then, to my horror, Auntie Blodwen, holding a document in her hand, came in herself to see my mother.

Before my last visit home to The Buildings I'd been given this piece of paper to take with me to be signed by my mother. Her signature was needed to certify that she gave her consent for me to ride a bicycle. Auntie Blodwen wanted to know if the signature was really my mother's. My mother put on her reading glasses, something I'd never seen her do.

'No,' she said, shaking her head. 'I don't remember signing this. This isn't my signature.'

She showed it to my stepfather. 'This isn't my signature, is it?'

'Nah,' he said.

My heart sank.

Auntie Blodwen's spirits seemed to rise.

But then my mother said, 'Hold on a bit, tell a lie . . . Yerst. I remember now. Terry asked me to sign this for him. That's right.'

Auntie Blodwen withdrew to the office, hopes raised and dashed.

Pop was in the office, too, smoking a pipe. I knew he was smoking because of the known reek of the tobacco. Visitors weren't allowed to smoke and the injustice didn't escape me. I put my ear to the partition wall, not caring that my mother and stepfather saw me. I was trying to be clever in front of them.

'It *is* her signature,' I heard Auntie Blodwen say.

'I told you so,' said Pop. 'The boy isn't that cunning.'

I sat down facing my mother and stepfather, but they had nothing to say and I began to panic and feel uncomfortable. The other groups in the room seemed to be functioning naturally. The awkward silence was suddenly broken by Pop. For once, I was glad to see him.

He came into the playroom, approached us and, taking his pipe out of his mouth, said to my mother that he understood she played the piano.

'Yerst,' she said. 'I can knock out a tune. What's it to you?'

Pop must have been surprised by the coarse tone in her voice, but without flinching and without answering her question immediately he said, 'Nonsense, you're being modest. I understand you play very well. Fishy told us.' He glanced down at me. 'Didn't he . . .?'

My mother flinched, looked at my stepfather, looked at me, and then looked at Pop again.

'I love the piano,' Pop continued. 'We have a very good one in the dining-room.'

'Who's Fishy?' my stepfather asked.

I sat there watching and listening. I wasn't happy about the way Pop was looking at my mother. He was looking at her in the same way that the lorry driver had looked at Patricia, and it crossed my mind what Pop might do to my mother.

'I'm a pianist, too,' Pop said. 'I must come to the pub to hear you play. We have a lot in common.'

'Fishy told you about the pub too, did he? How come?'

'He come to clean the windows,' I said.

'Who's Fishy?' my stepfather asked again.

After a few minutes Pop moved along and struck up a conversation with another group of visitors. I played with my fireman, but there was no rapport between us. Being visited by my mother had turned my thoughts to the anger and unhappiness of The Buildings. Maybe my new fireman friend knew about the loneliness and the abuse and the absence of laughter, and that's why there were so many pauses in the conversation between us. A huge blaze had taken hold that neither of us was equipped to deal with. The best we could hope to achieve was to limit the damage. My whole future was to become a damage limitation exercise. I just hoped my new fireman friend would stick by me. I held on to him tightly.

14

The Rub-a-Dub-Dub

I knew that Pop would go to the pub sooner or later to see my mother and I kept an eye on him. How he knew which pub to go to has always remained a mystery to me. The other thing that's puzzling is the measure of an old man's fondness for a middle-aged mother who is not his wife.

He made his move one Friday evening, announcing he was going to the Majestic cinema to see Alec Guinness in *Bridge Over the River Kwai*. I knew this was nonsense because *Around the World in 80 Days* was showing.

I made arrangements with the other children for my absence to be covered, and when Pop left I got my bike out and followed him. He caught a bus. As it was the end of the week, there was some traffic congestion and I managed to keep up with the double-decker relatively effortlessly until eventually the East End streets became familiar again.

Suddenly there in front of me was The Angel. The bus stopped and Pop alighted.

The pub never had looked especially inviting from the outside and nothing had changed. On the contrary, through my more experienced eyes, I thought it looked seedier than ever. But Pop had apparently made up his mind and he went through the double-hinged doors and into the Saloon Bar.

I parked my bike and listened and watched through the crack between the pub doors. It was years since I had looked in, and the Saloon Bar, though still large to my eyes, seemed to have shrunk a little. It looked as run-tight as ever in there. The ceiling was desperately in need of a coat of paint, the walls were still covered with the same dark-patterned paper, and there was my mother still sitting at the piano with her back to me. I felt no sense of achievement at having found her.

There were a number of tables in the room and the revellers were huddled round them, clutching their pints and loudly enjoying the human intercourse, ordinary down-to-earth types who exhibited no outward sign of taking themselves seriously.

Pop sat down on a stool at the bar and found himself in the company of several other men. One of them doffed his cap. Sitting by the door were two old mums, their purses on the table and their coats clutched to them. I recognised their wizened faces. They nodded their respects to Pop. It was amazing the effect a white collar and tie had on people in those days. Pop glanced again at the cap-doffer and nodded a belated salute. There was another doff of the cap with a small hand.

The governor made his way to Pop's end of the bar, the same governor I had known. After all this time, the same faces in the same places, symbols of stability in my life. He began to mop up with a dishcloth. The bar didn't need mopping; the action was a publican's reflex which ended as soon as Pop ordered his drink. The governor brought him something in a small glass and, mopping up again, started talking to the cap-doffer. 'Bev and me are thinking of going to Benidorm for a holiday.'

'Where's that?' the cap-doffer enquired.

'Costa del Sol. Guaranteed sun, good food, and drink. Ha ha.'

Pop was ready now to turn around and face my mother. She had her back to the audience and had placed Joe's old cheese-cutter cap on top of the bass key-block where everybody could see it, an old cap belonging to a new man.

She was now ready to play. There was no self-consciousness.

Without any introductions or fine words, she began. She would impress everybody with her hands, not with her tongue. But the real difficulty for her was to make herself heard above the laughing and joking and general background noise. She hung in there, balanced on the piano stool like a roll of emotional wallpaper, and in spite of everything my heart bled for her.

But before long everybody started to join in singing: 'When I Touched Me Seaweed I Knew It Was Gonna Be Wet'. She had got the measure of them at last. I knew the song, but Pop evidently did not. He was like Daniel, learning the language and literature of Babylonia while in exile, except Daniel had the gift of understanding. This was another world, of coarse laughter and people slopping cheap ale around. Gradually, in ones and twos, people stood up and started dancing. Every so often I would push one of the heavy, cumbersome doors open a little to get a better look. 'Gertcha,' someone would growl. 'Gertcha.'

It was getting busier by the minute and I found myself having to move away from the doors more often, to allow people through.

'Gertcha,' a familiar voice said to me. 'Gertcha.' I hoped he wouldn't tell anyone I was outside.

'It must be difficult to get drunk in here,' a stranger said to Pop, as he waited patiently at the bar to be served, at least that's what I thought he said.

'I'm sure you don't mind waiting,' Pop said, struggling to know how to respond.

'I don't mind waiting,' said the stranger, sticking his elbow into somebody close behind him, 'so long as everybody takes his turn.'

My mother looked round at last and noticed Pop. She smiled. He nodded in acknowledgment and she continued to play without taking her eyes off him. She eventually returned her gaze to the piano keys and was hard at it, playing a variety of tunes, for at least half an hour ('High Noon'/'Giddy-up-a-Ding-Dong'/'Deep Purple'/'A Dream Is a Wish Your Heart Makes'/'Again'/'On a Slow Boat to China'/'Walk Right In'/'You Belong to my Heart'/'Never Do a Tango with an Eskimo'/'Alright, Okay, You Win') and many more, before fighting her way to the bar and taking a well-earned break.

'What'll it be?' Pop said, putting his hand into his pocket. He had pride of place at the bar and was served quickly. My mother emptied her glass of its transparent liquor. They stood talking. I couldn't hear a word of what they said, but through the rabble I could read their wet lips and minds.

Then I was shocked to see Joe, fighting his way through the crowd with his crutches, heading in my direction towards the exit doors.

I retreated to the other side of the road. He came out of the pub and lurched off into the darkness, capless.

As soon as the doors had stopped swinging on their hinges, I went back to my station and spied again. There was hand-clapping and one or two cheers as my mother returned to the piano. 'Give us "We'll Meet Again", Emily,' cried a voice. She did as she was asked.

By ten-to-eleven there were a number of drinks lined up on top of the piano, the supply being greater than the demand and causing a tailback. My mother lifted another to her lips and tilted her head back until the glass was quite dry. Then, standing up, she took Joe's old cheese-cutter cap from the bass key-block, emptied the hat's contents into her handbag, and went round taking a further collection.

I knew she'd had a whip-round with a hat many times before and I supposed that it required some nerve, and that it might have helped if she kept in mind what she needed the money for

– unpaid rent, for example. It must have been difficult for her, but she seemed to concentrate her mind on what she was doing and Joe's cheese-cutter cap filled with money. Magic!

The governor was evidently pleased with the way the evening had gone and I saw him toss a number of silver coins into Joe's cap – three half-crowns maybe, 'half-dollars' as they were known in the East End of London at the time, that's 7/6d in old money. 'See you tomorrow?' he said. He was getting value for money and he knew it.

My mother thanked him, in her own impassioned, cliché-ridden, Cockney vernacular. Moving along, arm outstretched, she tried to give the impression to the line of meaner men who were propped up by the bar that it was as painful for her to take their hard-earned cash as it was for them to part with it.

Whenever my mother played the piano in a pub, money was put into the hat for a number of reasons. There were those people, for example, who enjoyed what my mother did, thanked her, and gave in the same way that they would pay for any service that was provided for their enjoyment. Others felt sorry for her and put something in because they thought she was worse off than she actually was. Others were confused and over-tipped accordingly, or didn't tip at all. And then again there were those who thought she had courage, and gave for no other reason than that they thought courage should be rewarded. The worst type in my mother's book were those who looked down their noses, as they might look down on a beggar, and tossed a farthing to save face. I wonder what marvellous things these fellow creatures themselves did for a living that they could afford to condescend to a busker.

The important thing was that most people gave generously. Of course, there were always one or two through the course of an evening who would enjoy themselves thoroughly, singing and dancing, asking for this tune and that, and then refuse point-blank to put their hands into their pockets. But they were few and far between. The lighter side of human nature being what it is, the majority of the drinkers actually enjoyed watching the hat being filled with money, even if some of it was their own. They enjoyed giving. It made them feel good. They were ragged-trousered philanthropists.

Pop reacted with a heart of gold and contributed a liberal number of silver coins. One or two others were less willing because they had put something into the hat on so many previous occasions that the ritual for them had become tedious. They warmly said 'hello' to my mother and praised her talent.

My mother looked more than pleased with the sum of money and returned to the piano for several encores ('Baby it's Cold Outside'/'All I Do is Dream of You'/'Ballad of Davy Crockett'/ 'The Poor People of Paris'/'Once in Love with Amy'/'We'll Meet Again').

At the eleventh hour the governor knew he could not bend the licensing law any further and he flashed the house lights on and off several times in quick succession to signal that the evening had come to an end. The cap-doffer went round collecting the last of the empty glasses and emptying the contents of used ashtrays into a metal bin, calling 'Time' as he went.

'Come on,' he said to the drinkers. 'Time. We've got your money. Now piss-orft home.' They did, ordering quarts of light or brown ale to take with them. I moved aside into the shadows as the drinkers came out.

On the corner they paused at Tubby Isaacs to buy seafood. They sang at the tops of their voices as they ordered winkles, whelks and jellied eels.

'Oi! Hold your noise down there. I've got to get up in the

morning,' cried a voice from the fourth floor of a building. The seafood-eaters took no notice.

Pop eventually brought my mother out of there and walked her to the bus stop, and there I saw them embrace each other like a pair of drunken fools. They caught a night bus and I followed on my bike. She was sitting next to the window, upstairs, he in the aisle seat. After the heat of the pub they looked grateful for the fresh air that blew over them through the half-open window. I pedalled hard, made sure they didn't see me following, and tried to think of something positive about my mother's piano playing but, no, it was awful.

And she was too old to learn. She was an actress, an entertainer. What she did was good, but it wasn't *music*, not in the true sense of the word. There were no what Pop would have called 'combinations of sounds'. There was only an endless decomposed rhythm. But it worked. My mother's handbag was heavy with the collection.

The bus pulled up at my mother's stop and they alighted and continued the last leg of the journey on foot.

Catching my breath in the shadows, I now pedalled at a snail's pace behind them.

'Best not to come any further. My husband might see you,' my mother said in the darkness, after hundreds of drunken steps.

There in front of us were the silhouettes of The Buildings, the flats in the sky.

On the spur of the moment Pop pulled my mother into one of the dark, ground-floor entrances. 'Come in here a minute,' I thought I heard him say. Blind drunk, he was right beside her. She was pressed against the wall.

Council-built flats in the sky were council-built flats in the sky. They had a strict uniformity of shape, colour and smell.

Strictly speaking, they were drained of colour. The passages were short and always smelled fiercely of soap and dust, and the doors and windows were mass-produced in a factory.

The ledged-and-battened door of the pram-cupboard was open wide, its lock broken as a matter of course. Even here, sex was endorsed by the presence of a pram-cupboard.

I was sitting on my bike in Belmont Road, no more than half a dozen shadows away. The air was so unclean that I almost lost my balance in the panic to get my index finger under my nose so that the itchiness in my nostrils would not end in a loud sneeze.

Pop hurried to satisfy his number one need. First he put his hand on my mother's neck, meditatively. My mother was waiting, one hand on his hip, the other clutching the pram-cupboard door by its edge. Then as an afterthought Pop had the bright idea of taking her right into the pram-cupboard. He led her inside under the concrete stairs and mercifully closed the door behind him.

$E = MC^2$. The matter of sex converted into pure energy. Ruled by a kind of anarchy, theirs was the dark love of the pram-cupboard, romance rather than any dazzling abstract ideal, the complete opposite of family loyalty, which is another kind of love and that finds full expression in marriage and parenthood. They had chosen this επιθυμια the Greek word for opportunists' desires for things that were not theirs – in other words, lust.

A waning gibbous moon followed me through Snaresbrook, across Wanstead Flats, past couples on parked motorbikes with side-cars, and all the way back to the children's home. No matter how fast I pedalled, I couldn't shake off the moon and it was still with me as I free-wheeled down Church Road.

The lights were still on in one or two houses. I parked my bike at the back of the home and went in through the back door, which had been left unlocked by Trevor. The dog whimpered behind the closed playroom door, and Sally the rabbit thumped the floor of her hutch as I silently crept upstairs. I knew which floorboards to avoid stepping on.

I halted outside Auntie Agnes's bedroom on the middle landing. I would sometimes stand there during the night, listening as Auntie Agnes revealed secret desires to Auntie Blodwen – Auntie Blodwen, another victim of nature's tricks, endowed with a rich intellect, her only compensation.

Auntie Blodwen and Auntie Agnes were resigned to the fact that they would never meet a man they would want to live with. In fact, it went beyond resignation; it was designation. They had found their niche in each other.

I went to bed and lay awake for I don't remember how long, my thoughts turning to Angela, Pia, Betty, Christine, Knighton Woods, Lady Linda's field, anybody or any place, so long as I could free my mind of the day's events. My open, rolling eyes came to rest on Trevor as he lay in bed. Then I fell asleep.

I opened my eyes innocently enough and then narrowed them beneath a frown. Why did my mother hate me? The others were still sleeping: Eddy restless, Trevor troubled, George blissfully as usual. I got out of bed. The reek of Pop's pipe was lingering on the landing. He was back. I went to the bathroom and began the ritual of washing pink hands and face with white soap and cleaning white teeth with pink powder. I was choked. I felt that Pop had not only abused my mother, but me too.

I felt I had to do something. It was Saturday and I confronted him in the dining-room after breakfast. He was alone playing the piano. He'd sat himself down and was playing solemnly, with a horrible look on his face. I started to speak.

'Sssshhh, I'm composing,' he said.

'Decomposing more like it,' I shouted.

He stopped playing and turned towards me. 'What did you say?'

I went over to him and thumped the keys of the piano as hard as I could with both hands. Then I ran into the garden and climbed to the top of the silver birch.

I had a good deal on my mind for a ten-year-old, but it was hard to make sense of anything. My mother was so different from Pop. Her life was out of control with so many special needs, whereas Pop seemed fairy-like on top of everything. At the time, I suppose, my mother would have been labelled 'educationally subnormal'. Pop was well educated, and that's what would have given appeal to his advances. My mother was demonstrably child-like in many ways, even to the point of my realising that at some stage of my childhood, incredible as it might sound, I would be expected to look after her rather than the other way round. She could barely read or write except to sign for something on hire purchase and she was perfectly willing to lean on anybody who would lend support.

While I sat on a thin branch compartmentalising, Elvis went to Number One with 'All Shook Up', Sputnik-1 circled above my head, without the world ending with a bang, and the disagreeable memory of my outing to the pub was bundled up at the back of my mind somewhere. And then Christmas was on top of us again.

Christmas Day was one day in the year we couldn't help but look forward to.

15

Christmas Observed

I awoke to find a full Christmas stocking on the end of my bed and Jenny romping around the room excited, ears pricked up. We couldn't believe it was Christmas Day at last.

Jenny barked and the other boys in my dormitory were awakened. We sat up and reached down to the ends of our beds, holding up the stockings and reaching inside.

I immediately pulled out a fountain-pen with a gold nib and I called across to the others. 'Look what I've got. Do you think the nib is real gold?'

'It looks like it,' Trevor said, looking over in my direction. 'Is there a carat marking on it?'

I looked everywhere.

George had found only tangerines in his stocking so far, but he was burrowing deeper, unperturbed, and eventually he found a watch that he placed on his wrist. Trevor had a new toothbrush and a racing car. Ricky was awake, but still lying down in bed, anaemic-looking and obviously not very well.

I went over to him, pen in hand. 'Do you think this nib is real gold?'

He got up on one elbow and looked closely at the nib. 'It looks like it,' he said. 'It's very shiny.' He lay down again.

'What's wrong with you?' I asked. 'It's Christmas.'

'I'm tired.'

I reached down for the stocking at the foot of his bed. 'Do you want me to see what's inside?'

He nodded his head and I began to empty the stocking of its contents.

Soon the bed was covered with pens, Dinky cars, sweets, chocolate, nuts, oranges, tangerines, wrapping paper and a small card portraying the baby Jesus. Christmas cards from lost parents were usually the ones that were secular, betraying Auntie Blodwen's professed bedrock belief; this one was from Father Worthington, but I couldn't work out why Ricky should be singled out this year in this way.

I put on my dressing-gown and, taking as many of my presents with me as I could carry, I joined the girls in one of the adjacent dormitories. George followed me in.

Auntie Blodwen was sitting on the end of Constance's bed, as charming as you like and being shown the contents of a stocking: dolls, sweets, chocolate, fruit, nuts and small toys and things. I showed Auntie Blodwen my pen and, sitting down on the bed, asked if she thought the nib was made of real gold.

She stood up. 'Of course it isn't. It's cheap, gold-coloured paint. It's time for breakfast. Come on, let's have you. Get washed, dressed and downstairs, immediately.' She led the way out of the dormitory.

George placed his new watch against his good ear and Christmas ticked away. We were dying with the ecstasy of it. Even Auntie Blodwen couldn't stop us enjoying ourselves.

We washed quickly, then returned to the dormitories to dress. Before going downstairs, I helped Ricky out of bed and took him to the bathroom. I helped him wash and dress and then we went downstairs together. The contents of his stocking remained strewn across his bed.

The dining-room was full of decorations again. They were not dead or dying; they had been hibernating. But where? The

Christmas tree was in its bucket in the corner, spruced up and reaching out with more presents for all of us.

The tablecloth was blue and covered with red napkins. Even the bread on the tables was different shades of brown and white. Everything had colour. I took a large box of chocolates with my name on them from under the tree, their insides were pink and green, and although Auntie Blodwen did look across at me, nothing was said as I brought them to the breakfast table and continued to munch them.

On Christmas Day I was happy for a while. Heaven was lying about me in pretty wrapping paper, and for a day I had a father, with a long white beard and a long red great-coat.

The Pope spoke on television of the need to suspend nuclear test explosions and the Queen made her Christmas Television debut, while an unknown person dressed as Father Christmas handed us gifts and made us smile. He looked like a demi-god in his mythical clothes. He gave each of us two small presents from his sack, but Vera wasn't too pleased with one of the gifts she was handed, and she reached up and pulled his beard off in disgust. With the loss of his whiskers, the divine hero also lost his temper and lunged out at her, the remaining contents of his sack spilled over the floor.

For the quiet, withdrawn Zsa Zsa it was a tense time because she wasn't going back to the same school. She was going to live with one of her parents in a flat in the sky. Who knew where the other parent was? Perhaps he was dead. She blamed herself for everything that was wrong in her life. She had confided in me that her mother hated her.

On Boxing Day she walked up and down the back garden waiting for going-home time. Jenny and I watched from beneath the sycamore, curiosity in the dog's eyes and sadness in mine. Pop, looking like a patriarch in his three-piece suit, glanced curiously from the closed landing window on the first floor as he made his way back to the sick-room. Zsa Zsa's skin was as pale as ever, but her brown hair now had a yellow light in it. She held a carrier bag in one hand and in the other a shoebox, and looked a proper little orphan. She was fully developed and her hazel eyes were almost wide open at last. The final preparations for her departure had been made and it was just a question now of waiting for the hour. Some of us would wave goodbye from the garden gate as she left for the Underground station with her bag and box. That was the most she could hope for. She had not been unpopular; it was simply that Auntie Blodwen made sure that emotion and sentimentality were guarded against. When the hour came, Zsa Zsa and I went from the back garden into the house and then Zsa Zsa stood by the front door.

'Do you have your train fare ready?' Auntie Blodwen asked.

'Yes, thank you, Auntie Blodwen.'

'It's a pity you couldn't have gone yesterday.'

'Isn't anybody coming to fetch you?' I asked, walking alongside Zsa Zsa as she went through the front door for the last time.

'Of course nobody's coming to fetch her, you idiot,' Auntie Blodwen said to me. 'Who do you think is going to come and fetch her on Boxing Day?'

Zsa Zsa shook her head, smiled bravely at me, and left the home in the same undignified fashion in which she had lived there. I followed her along the garden path and Andrew, darting from the house, joined us as an afterthought.

Zsa Zsa's figure grew smaller as she walked down the road towards the station. 'Goodbye, Zsa Zsa,' we called after her.

The following day Auntie Gladys passed plain hard-boiled eggs through the service hatch for tea and we knew that Christmas was over. A year was a long time. The Christmas decorations were still up, but there were no more nice things to eat, no more stuffed chicken or mince pies with custard. We were brought down to earth with a boiled egg. The atmosphere had changed. The hard-leafed holly with red berries had disappeared from both tables, and lighted candles between bunches of multi-coloured flowers were no longer to be seen. I raised an eyebrow in Pia's direction and the eggs kept coming.

With hard-boiled eggs inside us, we spent the evenings in the playroom reducing jigsaw puzzles to order, playing pick-a-stick, and making dinosaurs out of papier mâché. Our Christmas prayer was that Auntie Blodwen would not come out of the office and interrupt the relative calm.

When I returned to school my class was getting ready for the run-up to the eleven-plus exam. This would determine the type of secondary school I should go to. It was a foregone conclusion that I would fail, and so I tried to turn it into a joke. I had a poor image of myself as a pupil, and that had to be made funny to be bearable.

I was beaten at the children's home and spat on and called names at school by parented classmates. No physical giant (I was probably a little below average weight and height), I learned at an early age that I could make my tormentors laugh with a sense of humour that was instinctive in a hostile environment.

On more than one occasion Mr Thomas asked me if I was going to be a comedian when I left school. Although I've never ventured down that road, the comic's vocation is one that has always appealed to me.

I passed my eleventh birthday, but failed my eleven-plus. What a joke that was.

16

Secondary Modern School

As the date of the eleven-plus exam approached, my jokes became more desperate.

'Ask me if I like geometry,' I said to Paul Worthington, one day in the playground.

'*Do* you like geometry?' he obliged.

'No,' I said. 'I can't see the point.'

Up until the last moment, I was cracking them. On the day, I remember standing outside the examination hall with the other candidates and asking if anyone knew how the Grand Canyon was formed.

The other boys in Mr Thomas's class ignored me, but a boy from another school near Chigwell thought I was being serious.

'I say, do you think we'll be asked that question?'

'Well, you never know,' I said. 'It's geography, innit?'

'That's enough, Denby. This is hardly the time,' Worthington said, nervously.

A teacher then opened the doors to the examination hall and we were asked to go in and find our places.

'The Grand Canyon was hollowed out by the Colorado River, wasn't it?' the boy from Chigwell said, as we made our way inside.

'Nah,' I replied. 'A Scotsman was there on holiday and he lost his wallet.'

The boy stood still between the desks for a moment and scrutinised me.

'Think about it,' I said.

I found my place and sat down. I didn't have a clue how to answer any of the questions and failed miserably. This meant I would go to a secondary modern school to complete my education in September of that year, 1958.

I wasn't, of course, the only one who failed in Mr Thomas's class. Out of thirty boys, I think about seventeen of us failed. In fact, at the time it wasn't a question of passing or failing in a strict sense. Political will was directed at the regulation of the flow of primary-school children into grammar schools. If you want 20 per cent to go there, you award the eleven-plus to the appropriate number of children. The government wanted only a certain number of pupils to go on to grammar school, so it only let a certain number through, those with the highest marks. But there was no line drawn that said, *this* is where you pass and *this* is where you fail. It wasn't a question of achieving a prescribed level of attainment; it was a question of being among the best. It didn't matter how clever you were and how hard you worked; if there were enough candidates taking the exam who were a fraction better than you, you risked going to a secondary modern.

For me, the method of selection was irrelevant because I was never going to pass anyway, but for some pupils and their families it caused a great deal of dissatisfaction. The problem arose because of the bulge in the number of eleven-year-olds, and the prospect ultimately of too many children chasing too few jobs. In 1958 in Great Britain, in round figures, 650,000 children reached the age of fifteen and the figure was rising.

If you went to a secondary modern school there were no means of gaining academic qualifications such as 'O' levels and 'A' levels, and so you were destined for some kind of vocation, such as bricklayer, painter and decorator or motor mechanic. On the other hand, if you passed the eleven-plus and went on to grammar school the sky was the limit, literally, you could become a pilot, enter civil aviation or the RAF, or you could become a solicitor, a teacher, a doctor and even a priest if you had the right calling. Or you could go into politics. Why not?

I now had the six-week summer holiday in front of me to reflect on my future vocation. What would *I* rather be? A lorry driver or a builder's labourer? A stevedore or a boiler cleaner? A steel erector's mate or a bus driver? A dustman or a road sweeper? A navvy or a factory worker? Or would I follow in my stepfather's footsteps and become a public lavatory attendant?

Was there no real hope of anything for me beyond childhood other than a factory floor or the cavernous subterranean abode of a public lavatory? Would a public lavatory, for me, be the end of life's journey? I know there's no shame in doing manual work, in holding down an honest job to support a family and to give children the best upbringing possible and start in life within limited means. At the poorest levels of society parents keep their children clean, shower them with love, and help with school homework in the hope that one day the kids might be able to escape impoverishment. These parents have dignity and self-respect. But it's wrong, because of a political agenda, to limit, when there is no actual poverty of choice, a young person's career options at the tender age of eleven where there is so much unknown potential for great things.

Wimbledon Lawn Tennis Championship was in full swing and Auntie Blodwen and Auntie Agnes spent a great deal of time in front of the television. I couldn't understand why they became so excited. Sitting and watching somebody hit a ball with a racket was so alien to me. I couldn't for the life of me imagine anyone round The Buildings being motivated, or having the inclination, or even the time, to sit and watch anybody do such a thing. Wimbledon was so middle class, with its champagne and strawberries; definitely not for the likes of us. There were no short, lace-trimmed tennis skirts in 1958; they would have been considered vulgar and even sinful – though the wearing of such clothes might just have stimulated my interest in tennis and provoked me into watching.

Whatever motivated her, Auntie Blodwen would put her thick-rimmed spectacles on, sit opposite Auntie Agnes and be glued to the screen, her eyes shifting from left to right behind those thick lenses, following each and every trajectory of the ball. Auntie Blodwen and Auntie Agnes both would be wearing soberly practical loose-fitting skirts almost down to their ankles, garments that hung so loosely on them they seemed to touch neither the waist nor hips.

Another vital statistic I find interesting is that most Wimbledon watchers in the 1950s were in the higher income bracket. I don't know if the same is true today.

Ashley Cooper won the men's singles that year, with a wooden racket in those days, of course, but the African-American, Althea Gibson, was making an even greater impact on the tennis world, successfully defending her singles title and doing so much to break down class and racial barriers.

I preferred to listen instead to pop music, but it wasn't easy. We benighted children still relied on an old, wind-up gramophone, a battered pile of scratched 78 rpm records, and a dwindling supply of needles. The Everly Brothers were in the charts, but I seem to remember they were censored by Auntie Blodwen. 'You Need Hands' by Max Bygraves was one of those songs that escaped her censorship and we made do with Max for much of the holiday; 45 rpm singles and 33 rpm long-players were out there somewhere, but we never saw them, and woofers and tweeters were definitely not yet part of our vocabulary.

In September I went to the local secondary modern school and the same old pattern began to repeat itself. I had no motivation, I understood absolutely nothing about what went on in the classroom, and I was disruptive and undisciplined. I was often punished – and these days I always deserved it.

Whatever arguments were in vogue at the time for single-sex education, this was a mixed school; it was girls and boys in the same classroom together, and I became aware immediately of the different attitudes the teachers had towards girls and boys. Although I was badly behaved and hardly ever did any work, I was no longer the consummate underdog; I had a degree of status, I was a boy. Even when I was disruptive, the teacher seemed to be more responsive to my interjections.

I suppose the teachers in those days thought they were educating girls and boys for different roles in life, assuming a domestic role for the girls because they lacked the assertiveness necessary to succeed in anything other than washing, ironing and darning socks. The downside to being valued as a boy was that more was expected of me. But not always. Sometimes I was let off for not participating, while the female half of the class was encouraged to perform. 'Come on, girls, you must have some ideas on this too,' the teacher used to say, patronisingly.

Outside and away from school the girls were now too old to play with the new Barbie dolls that were being introduced at the time, but the more adventurous ones were latching on to Espresso coffee, Wimpy bars and stereo music. Teddy Boys were still a force to be reckoned with, but they were mutating into Rockers.

The ultra-conservative Pope Pius XII was dead, liberal Pope John XXIII was newly elected, and before long the drug

Thalidomide would be blamed for birth defects; the period also witnessed the emergence of the 'modern' teenager.

Oh Boy! was on Independent Television, produced by Jack Good, who had left *Ready Steady Go*; and the programme was shot by Geoff Sanders, ABC Television's senior cameraman at the time. I managed to catch a glimpse of the show at somebody's house if I dared stay out late on a Saturday. When I returned to the children's home I would be in deep trouble with Auntie Blodwen, of course, but sometimes I couldn't help myself. My favourite act was in fact the show's resident house band, Lord Rockingham's XI, with their single called 'Hoots Mon' ('There's a moose loose aboot this hoose')! What did that make me? What was this predilection for Lord Rockingham's XI?

I still didn't have a clue who or what I was. I'd long since lost my identity; I was invisible. Would I grow up to be a Mod or a Rocker? Or something in between? A Mocker? Would I ride a Triumph 650cc to work? Or a Vesper GS? Or something middle of the road?

For better or worse, after less than a year, uncontrollable events of an exquisitely personal nature were about to lead me away from my secondary school. The spring term was to be my last and I didn't even see the end of that. On my last day at the school, 19 March 1959 and a Thursday, I received six of the best from the Headmaster for birds'-nesting in the trees lining the school's playing fields. Some of the other pupils grassed on me and I felt really humiliated and worthless because they were my friends. To make things worse, the Headmaster stood me in front of the whole school and explained to everybody what I had done before taking me to his office and giving me what-for.

He swished the cane through the air before asking me to

bend over and, as he hit me and hit me, I listened to a running commentary on his perception of the type of person I was.

'You're from Gibblings Shaw, aren't you?'

Swiiish.

'Beginning to find your feet at this school, are you, young man?'

Swiiish.

'Coming out in your true colours, at last?'

Swiiish.

'I'll teach you to go *birrrds*'-nesting.'

Swiiish.

'You little nose-rag.'

Swiiish. Swiiish.

To this day, I don't know why I wanted to take those eggs.

Nobody knew it was to be my last day. The Headmaster and the birds had nothing to do with my leaving. The unrelated events leading up to my being taken away began to unfold that evening.

17

Auntie Blodwen's Wicked Imagination

When I returned to Gibblings Shaw a little before five o'clock, the trouble I was in at school was common knowledge and it had put Auntie Blodwen into a particularly nasty mood. The look she gave me said everything. At the table in the dining-room I could hardly sit still to have my tea because of my discomfort from the caning, and after tea when everybody else was sitting down watching television, I was walking up and down in the playroom holding my bottom. With only the dog for company, I stopped pacing up and down and knelt on the floor to pat her.

Then, Auntie Blodwen came into the playroom and I watched nervously as she silently closed the door behind her. She walked straight over to me. I turned white as I looked up at her.

'Leave the dog alone,' she said. 'Haven't you caused enough trouble for one day?' Grabbing my hair, she cried: 'Leave the dog alone.'

'I was only patting her' I wanted to say, but before I could get the words out of my mouth, she brought her knee up under my chin, using such force that my whole body was lifted from the floor. She let me fall on to the carpet in front of her, and with an outstretched arm pointed the finger at me. 'Leave the dog alone.'

I lay on the floor, heaving, holding my face in my hands. My head felt as if it were split in two. The rest of the evening remains a complete blur to me.

When I went up to bed, I couldn't sleep. I lay awake squinting through the window at a cluster of familiar stars. I wondered if they really existed. I imagined they didn't, that they were spots on the window glass waiting for the chamois leather, or pawns on a galactic chessboard, vying for position around the Earth Queen. I pulled the bedclothes irritably under my swollen chin and eventually dropped off to sleep.

Friday 20 March 1959

I woke early and listened to the clatter of milk bottles as the milkman coaxed his float up the hill. It was still dark. I slipped out of bed, put my dressing-gown on, and quietly made my way downstairs to the playroom.

Jenny was awake and jumped out of her basket. She came over to me and licked my toes. Then together we went along the corridor to the kitchen and through the scullery into the larder. I opened the refrigerator door and looked around inside for something nice to eat. I don't remember feeling particularly hungry whenever I raided the refrigerator. It wasn't a question of hunger. As a child, I wasn't in fact particularly interested in food. Perhaps the urge for extra food sometimes during the night was a psychological need because a full stomach somehow made me feel less insecure? I don't know. I'm not a child psychologist.

Jenny, on the other hand, was a hunting dog and she would woof down anything, anytime, day or night. She must have known Auntie Blodwen had come downstairs and was standing behind us, but the food was too much of a distraction and she ignored her presence and gave no danger signal.

I had my head in the refrigerator. I looked round eventually, sensing something. I closed the refrigerator door meekly as I found myself gazing into Auntie Blodwen's ogre face.

Without warning she kicked me between the legs, and with a cry I doubled up in indescribable pain. She always hit hard and fast, when and where you didn't expect it.

'Having an early breakfast?' she asked, and then she kicked me again and seemed to lose control, her anger bubbling over as she rained blows down on me.

I collapsed on to the larder's concrete floor and tried to protect myself by curling up into a ball. I knew it was futile to try and fight back. I just lay there, gritting my teeth.

Jenny had long since made good her escape when Auntie Blodwen took hold of me by the scruff of the neck, manhandled me into the kitchen and pushed me into a chair.

I have a vague memory of Auntie Agnes taking some cups and saucers from a cupboard, then walking past me into the scullery. Then I was aware of the other children looking through the service hatch to see what was going on.

'Jenny's upset,' I heard Pia say. 'She's in the boot-room whining.'

Auntie Blodwen came through from the scullery and, on her way to see to the dog, told me to go upstairs and get washed and dressed. I did exactly as I was told.

After breakfast, I was taken into the office and instructed to sit on the settee. Still anaesthetised from the kicking I had endured on the floor of the larder, her knee-jerk reaction in the playroom the previous evening, and the beating I had been given at school, I watched Auntie Blodwen's lips move and I could hear her voice. She was making accusations and asking questions that I didn't understand.

'You've been having sex with Jenny, haven't you?'

She came over to the settee, lifted me up on to my feet by the collar of my shirt, and held me there as she snarled in my face. 'Haven't you?'

I didn't react emotionally, as you might expect. I didn't care. I was past caring. In fact, it went beyond that. I was past, past caring. Was this another of their little jokes? A punishment gone wrong? Meted out by executioners who couldn't quite get it right? A botched job? Of course, I was afraid, but it was a numb kind of fear that could no longer express itself. I was miserable with uncertainty, at odds with everything, and open-mouthed. I was orphaned. The seed of zombie-ism was taking root in me and strangling me emotionally. There was very little dialogue. I had little to say.

And anyway, Auntie Blodwen's grip on my shirt collar was choking me. I heard myself trying to answer 'yes' and 'no' in what I thought were the right places. I was so afraid. All I wanted was to avoid another beating. I felt faint through lack of oxygen and the room was spinning. I would have told her anything she wanted to hear.

'I knew it!' I heard her exclaim, as she threw me in a heap back on to the settee.

I got my breath back and, in my confusion, began to experience my nightmare sensation. Heaviness was around me and ZZZZZZZ was in my ears and in my eyes. I was confused. You might expect me to have been disgusted, but I wasn't. And neither were they. To be disgusted at something one needs first of all to have a strong aversion towards that thing. As I looked up at Auntie Blodwen and Auntie Agnes, their eyes revealed something to me. It wasn't disgust they felt at all; there was something else behind their gaze, a different kind of aversion. And, as for me, since the idea of somebody having sex with a dog had never crossed my mind, never even come within a zillion, grillion miles of my eleven-year-old thought processes, why should I, on the spur of the moment, be disgusted? If I had been guilty, I would have been disgusted. But I was innocent. 'Disgust' is the wrong word. The point of departure for any attempt I make at explaining how I felt must be from the standpoint of innocence and fear.

Now, on one level, I can see the absurdity of an eleven-year-old boy having sex with a household pet. But at the time I didn't think it was absurd. Six years at Gibblings Shaw taught me not to think. And, what's more, Auntie Blodwen and Auntie Agnes, whatever their motives for making such a silly/horrific accusation, were in deadly earnest. Standing over me, scaring the shit out of me, Auntie Agnes backing up Auntie Blodwen, and confirming my guilt with pathetic remarks like 'He's got away with quite a few things since he's been here.'

They let me go.

The other children went to school and somehow I survived the next hour isolated upstairs in my dormitory. From the closed window I saw Auntie Gladys arrive and hurry through the garden. At about half-past nine Auntie Blodwen and Auntie Agnes came upstairs and collected me, and I left Gibblings Shaw for good.

I was marched down Church Road to the Underground station, the word 'home' now consummately more academic than homelessness itself.

When the train arrived, Auntie Blodwen jostled me into a smokers' carriage and I sat down opposite her as she lit a cigarette without taking her eyes off me.

We were on our way to the 'home office'. Less than half the seats were occupied, but still one or two people preferred to stand, hanging on to the leather straps that dangled above their heads. As the train trundled into London, I tentatively began to look around the carriage. I glanced sideways at some of the other passengers. They too must have been on their way to an event of some kind. Then I looked over the top of Auntie Blodwen's head and started to read the advertisements. Player's Weights. Who on earth thought up a name like that for cigarettes? *Eights*, yes. Then they could have been sold in packets of eight more competitively than other brands packaged in tens. We English Invaded Germany, Hitler's Troops Surrendered. The mnemonic was good.

I shifted my eyes. *In case of emergency, pull chain.* What was this, a train or a lavatory? *Penalty for improper use £5.* It was a train. Nobody paid £5 to spend a penny. Auntie Blodwen was still looking across at me. I could feel her eyes on me. *Aunt* Blodwen, I thought, and another mental process got under way in my mind.

We alighted at Stratford, found the Way Out sign, and passed through the ticket-barrier. Outside in the street it was raining. Auntie Blodwen opened her umbrella and we trod carefully over cobbled stones.

We were expected at the 'home office' and a man was waiting just inside the entrance as we arrived.

'You're not serious, are you?' These were his first, urgent words to Auntie Blodwen, before she'd even had time to close her umbrella.

'I know about the stories that went around after the war,' he continued, 'but he's only eleven.'

He asked Auntie Blodwen and Auntie Agnes to take a seat in the reception area and took me into his office. He didn't seem to know where to begin. Pushing my head to one side with his hand as a delaying tactic, he looked at the bruises on my face and neck. 'How did you get these bruises?' he asked. 'Have you been fighting?'

'No,' I said.

'How did you get them?'

'I fell when I was climbing a tree.'

'Do you know who I am?'

I shook my head, staring into space.

He turned away from me, sat down behind his desk, and instructed me to sit down opposite him. 'So, my boy, been up to no good, have you? You been doing things to Jenny?'

I lowered my head and breathed deeply.

'Ah, I thought so. How old are you? Eleven?'

'Twelve nearly.'

'Nearly twelve years of age. You really have let a lot of people down, including yourself. You can't go back to Gibblings Shaw.'

I nodded my head in agreement.

'Did anything come out of the end of your penis?'

I had never ejaculated in my life, but in an abused sort of way I suddenly felt grown-up, being spoken to like this. I knew what the man was talking about. This was men's talk.

'You'll have to go back to Boyles Court. There's nowhere else.'

I was afraid to tell him I hadn't done what I was being accused of. If I told him that, he might have sent me back to Gibblings Shaw.

18

Boyles Court Revisited

During my first stay at Boyles Court I hadn't fitted in because of my age. This time I was ten times more anomalous in my school blazer and gartered socks.

My first stay had been in 1953. Barely six years of age, I had arrived in rags, but apart from my young age, I hadn't looked out of place. Now I was different. There was something *black coat* about me.

The other boys were dressed in their institutional grey jackets and flannels, and they had been given a short back and sides by a visiting peripatetic barber. But they knew what was out there in the real world.

This was 1959. Children who were nearly twelve years old didn't walk around in short trousers and gartered socks unless there was something seriously wrong. As with popular music, fashion was loud. Teddy Boys were still affecting an Edwardian style of dress: drainpipe trousers with brightly coloured socks, slim Jim ties and long coats with velvet collars, cuffs and pocket flaps. And whether you were a Teddy Boy or an emerging, fledgling Rocker, hairstyles demanded long sideburns, with a quiff at the front and a DA ('ducks arse') at the back.

I'd recently been given a short back and sides at the children's home and there was nothing odd about that, but it was my clothes that stood out.

The other boys regarded me with ghoulish curiosity and the time-honoured question was thrown at me: 'Wha'd a' you up for?'

I really struggled to find the answer to this one. They insisted I come clean, but what crime had I committed? I'd been to court for being out of control or 'Beyond Control' and 'Exposed to Moral Danger', to quote accurately from section 61 of the Children's and Young Persons' Act of 1933. That was nearly six years ago, and not a very good professional reference in the criminal circle in which I again found myself.

'I came down in the night,' I said.

'Came down in the night?' queried a boy.

'Came down in the night,' mimicked another.

I felt uneasy. Something was putting them off liking me.

The boys searched one another's faces for an explanation. Perhaps this was new underworld jargon for something rational like 'Taking and Driving Away' or 'Grievous Bodily Harm'. It might be a new offence altogether, fresh on the statute book, something unmentionable. How were they to know? These young offenders' greatest fear was of losing one another's respect, and the surest way to do that was to appear out of touch. In the 1950s there wasn't much room for squares in criminal circles, so they looked at me and then at each other again, and then wandered off and kept well away from the eleven-year-old boy who wore short trousers and *came down in the night*. I might have murdered somebody.

I was taken upstairs, told to undress, and pushed under a cold shower. Then I was taken downstairs again and fitted out with socks and underwear, a jacket, long trousers and sturdy shoes. I'd been pushed around and kitted out like this for as long as I could remember by strange, unfriendly people, but I still couldn't get used to it. I was still afraid, not knowing what was going to happen next. The world remained a cold, frightening, military place.

'Get yourself over to the dining-room,' said the man who

had fitted me out. 'And be quick about it.' He started to give me directions.

'I know where it is,' I said. 'I've been here before.'

'Well *go* then,' he said. 'Don't just stand around talking about it.'

I trudged over to the dining-room in my heavy shoes and briefly re-examined the rooms and corridors on the way; even the tiniest nook was still familiar to me. I passed Mr Hobsbawm's office. He was sitting there with the door open, his famous sports jacket stretched tighter than ever around his back and shoulders. There was nothing Teddy Boyish about him. The light bulb with a green, metal shade was still dangling above his desk from the middle of the ceiling.

And then I saw Mr Graham coming towards me along the corridor. Still confused and in a dream, I looked down at the floor.

'Where are you off to?' he asked abruptly as he drew level with me.

I stopped, looked up and opened my mouth – not to speak, but in an involuntary gesture of bewilderment.

'It's teatime. You should be in the dining-hall.'

I stood with my mouth open, gaping up at him.

He stood looking down at me. 'God knows what will become of you after what you've done,' he said.

He didn't think Auntie Blodwen's accusation was silly, like any normal person would have done. He thought I was a monster.

'Don't you *care* what happens to you?'

'No,' I said.

It was the wrong answer. He clouted me round the back of the head with his hand. I didn't care; I was past that. Mr Graham was looking down on the outside of me, expecting to hear coherent, rational answers to his questions.

But inside I was numb. I had forgotten how to laugh even hollowly and the numbness inside me brought with it an end to tears. They just couldn't get out. Inside I was choking and it was an effort to speak. Having been falsely accused, I was now waiting for a responsible adult to come up to me and say: 'It's all right, Terry. We know you didn't do it. Nobody did it. Auntie Blodwen made a really silly mistake.' But that wasn't happening.

Mr Graham's violence endorsed the accusation and confirmed my guilt. He hit me round the back of the head again, harder this time, as if he were trying to knock some guilt into me. 'You *should* care what happens to you. Say something, boy. Don't you have anything to say for yourself?'

'I don't know what I'm supposed to say,' I said, my voice stuttering and trembling.

The second clout around the back of my head had the desired effect. I became emotional and started feeling guilty, for a crime I had not committed and for all sorts of other reasons.

He roughly pushed me in the direction of the dining-hall.

I stumbled forward, like a zombie, with my mouth open, and through the open windows of the corridors I noticed the views outside again. They were still the same as before despite the passing of the years. The same trees were growing in the same fields, the same species of insect flew and crawled, and I could still hear the rumble of traffic on the London Road, although it sounded closer now.

I entered the dining-hall. The food, the sausages and beans, was as predictable as ever; like the English weather, wet and meaningless with occasional bright spots.

After tea and another wash, I followed everybody into the room where the piano was, for hymn-singing. We sang our hymns and prayed and then they put me in the Indigo dormitory where the violet-coloured light shone above the inside of the door.

Lying in the metal-framed bed, for the first time in I don't know how long, I neglected to say my prayers before I went to sleep. Saying them had become such a routine, a habit, pure and simple. Instead, I thought of suicide and imagined how it might be achieved. Head in the gas oven was obviously the simplest and least painful. I would drift away.

My mother had always threatened she would do it, to me and to herself, and Jimmy had offered a mocking coin for the gas meter, daring her.

It would be a simple matter for me to creep down to the kitchen one night. I wouldn't need a coin to feed a stupid gas meter, only the guts to go through with topping myself, to turn the tap on, and then lie down with my head and shoulders in the oven. That would show them when they found me.

I really did think a voice was telling me to kill myself. I don't think I wanted to succeed. An attempt would be enough; it would be my way of manipulating them. *Look what you've pushed me to*, my deed or half-deed would cry up at them. My dead or half-dead body would make them sit up and listen – if not to me, then to other children. I didn't really want to die. I was scared of death, as most children are. I wanted help. I was becoming impulsive during a time of emotional upset; at last, a strong reaction to my loss of family and normal childhood. I wasn't that determined, I just didn't have a way out of that remand centre. A suicide attempt would be a call for help. I wanted to see my mother dead, not myself. It was her fault. The harder life became, the more I hated the woman who allowed it to happen and the more I wished her dead. I didn't blame Auntie Blodwen, not half as much as I blamed my mother. How could I? I didn't expect anything from Auntie Blodwen. She wasn't even a real aunt; she was nothing to me. But my mother was my own flesh and blood and children have a right to expect certain things from their parents.

My thoughts were secret. I would not breathe a word of them to anybody. How could I? Why shock people? The indigo light above the door burned all night.

A tedious time followed. I had lessons with an ageing Mr Graham in his cold classroom and there were the regular deliberately arduous supervised walks which tested my new cobbled boots to the point of no return. At the same time, arrangements were being made for me to see the child psychologist; not because anybody suspected me of being suicidal, but because of this *other business*.

19

The Child Psychologist

I found myself once again in Mr Hobsbawm's office. The child psychologist was seated opposite me behind the desk. Her jacket was, as always, neatly buttoned at the front and I imagined her skirt still to be slim and straight and her shoes pointed. The large window facing east was closed, but now a wooden ladder was leaning against the external sill.

The radiator! I laughed to myself as I looked at it. I felt I knew all its curves.

The child psychologist engaged me with a look and a smile and then began her interrogation of me. 'What do people usually call you? Is it Tell? Terry? Or Terence? How do you like to be addressed? What do your friends call you? Do you remember the last time I saw you, at the child guidance clinic?'

'Yes,' I said.

Saying 'yes' was problematical. There existed at the time a separation of the classes. I was working class, but occasionally I would meet someone who was middle class: a social worker, a doctor, a school inspector, a child psychologist; it was usually somebody in a clinical or administrative context. These encounters served to impress upon me how different I was and awakened feelings of inferiority, and I found myself trying to say 'yes' instead of 'yeah' and 'thank you' instead of 'fank you'. And I was forever saying 'pardon' whether I needed to apologise for something or not, because I was so used to always being made to feel in the wrong.

I remember that my mother's inferiority complex was

awakened too, when she chanced to meet these people, and she would sometimes blurt out 'yerst', a sort of interlarding of 'yes' and 'yup'. When I was old enough to understand, I found 'yerst' particularly inelegant. If anybody was within earshot, my cringe factor would go through the roof.

The child psychologist glanced down at the report she had made those five and a half years ago at the child guidance clinic in Plaistow and read quietly to herself, her lips hardly moving, something about 'unusual maturity traits' and my being 'excitable and uncontrolled' for my age. If I remember correctly, she continued: 'Terence, I'm going to say some words to you and I want you to tell me about the first thing that each word makes you think of. OK?'

'Yes,' I said, 'but don't call me Terence. My name is Terry.'

She continued her examination of me, asking questions, making notes, but it was difficult for me to find words to describe my feelings. After all those years in the children's home, my mind had become fuddled; I had learned not to think.

'Come on, Terry Denby,' she chivvied. 'Talking can be therapeutic. With questions and answers, nightmares locked up inside us can be dreamed in the cold light of day. Was it so bad at the children's home?'

I didn't know what to say.

'When is your birthday?'

That was easy. 'Twenty-third of April,' I said. 'Same day as Shakespeare.'

'Golly,' she said. 'Shakespeare.'

She took a breath and continued: 'I have a copy of your birth certificate right here in front of me. Your father's name and occupation are not given, but on your baptism certificate your alleged father's Christian names are recorded as Daniel William, yet the same document indicates that your father is unknown.

And your unknown father's "Quality, Trade or Profession" is shown to be that of a decorator. I find it all very confusing.'

'Think of what it must be like for me,' I said.

She looked up from her notes. 'Have you ever met your father?'

'Not as far as I know.'

'It's a wonder your mother didn't christen you *William* – I mean, you being born on the same day as Shakespeare.'

I shrugged my shoulders.

'Still, at least she had you christened. Was she superstitious?'

'I don't know,' I said. 'I don't remember anything about my christening. I was only a baby.'

'What were the first words you remember your mother saying to you?'

'Fuck Jesus.'

'Jesus!'

'And she used to call me an unnatural bastard.'

'That's a strange thing for a mother to call her son. Did she know something?'

I shrugged my shoulders.

'What about toys?'

'What about them?'

'Did you have any?'

'I had an aeroplane and a pedal car. But a rag-and-bone man passed by in the road one morning with his horse-and-cart and took my pedal car away. My mum called him upstairs from the open front-room window. She let him have it for half-a-crown. It was a nice car. Half-a-crown seemed a lot, though. I don't know what else she let him have, but I was speechless as he walked out of the flat with my pedal car under his arm.'

'Didn't your brothers and sisters have anything to say about that?'

'Some things are too painful to tell your brothers and sisters.'

'OK, Terry,' she said, 'I know what happened at the children's home and I think we should talk about it. First of all, I want you to tell me in your own words what you did.'

'I didn't do anything,' I said. 'Nobody will believe me, though.'

She interlocked her hands on the desk-top and continued: 'Were you unhappy at the children's home?'

Answering these questions wasn't easy, and not much help was forthcoming from the psychologist in formulating my personal persuasions about Gibblings Shaw. I enlightened her as best I could about Auntie Blodwen and Auntie Agnes, but I was still afraid to say too much. Instead I gave a description in terms of the house and garden, and after she had handed me a pencil and paper I made a consummate diagram of the sleeping arrangements.

'I was always getting into trouble and being blamed for things I didn't do,' I said, tentatively, handing over the diagram.

'Like this business with . . .' Her voice sounded almost sympathetic as it fell away.

'Yes. I wanted to leave and go back home and live with my mum. When my half-brother got married there was enough room for me, but Auntie Blodwen said that he'd taken his bed with him so it wasn't possible. So I started to save up for a bed. I used to leave for school early and run instead of catching the bus. I used to enjoy seeing how far I could get before the bus caught up and overtook me. Then all the kids on the bus would wave. I saved threepence a day like that. Then there was my pocket-money, it soon mounted up. I did a bit of cadging as well. It's surprising how much people will give if they think it's for a good cause. I don't know how much beds cost, but I must have had enough to buy a double one with knobs on when

Auntie Maxwell the cleaner found the money hidden in a box on top of the wardrobe.

'I let Auntie Blodwen and Auntie Agnes believe what they wanted to believe, that I'd stolen the money. They wouldn't take "no" for an answer. If they'd been real parents, they would have known I was telling the truth. They said I couldn't have saved all that money from not paying bus fares.'

I stopped talking, wondering how much I should reveal to this lady, but after a moment's hesitation I continued nevertheless: 'When I was at the children's home, I was in the end bathroom one evening, with Pia. We were supposed to be cleaning our teeth. I asked her if she would let me see her.'

'And?'

'She pulled her pyjama bottoms down and sat on the edge of the bath.'

'How old is Pia?'

'She's the same age as me.'

'Did you touch her?'

'Yes. I brushed my hand against her.'

'What you did with Pia was not bad, really,' the psychologist assured me. 'It's the sort of caper that many boys your age get up to. Your curiosity is typical for a boy your age. I don't think you should do anything like that again, mind you. It can get out of hand. Don't think that you've done anything terribly wrong on that score. But going back to this other business . . . The thing is, Terry, it does happen. Men, and yes, even young boys; there are known cases.'

'They must be mad,' I said.

'Why must they be mad?'

'Can I ask *you* a question?' I said, desperately, wanting to change the subject. 'Don't you think it's . . .'

The child psychologist was having none of that. 'Why must they be mad?' she repeated.

'There wouldn't be any point, would there? Unless they were mad.'

'There are known cases. In fact, bestiality is common in rural areas.'

'Is that what it's called?'

'Yes. Investigations have recently shown that about 17 per cent of farm boys from certain rural areas have had sexual contact with farm animals.'

'Why?'

'Why? Can you see any reason in biological terms for the confinement of sexual activity to contact between males and females of the same species?'

'What?'

'We know that sexual activity is usually confined to contact between males and females of the same species, but nobody knows why. We can't explain why an animal of one species doesn't mate or attempt to mate with other species of animal. It's not a question of why individuals of different species should be attracted to each other sexually. The pertinent question is why do individuals not regularly make contacts with species other than their own?'

'I still think a farm boy would be mad to go with an animal,' I said.

'Not really,' she answered. 'A farm boy would observe the sexual activities of animals daily. His response to watching them might be sympathetic. Moreover, if he sees other boys doing it, he might follow their example. He might not think he's doing anything really bad, just having some fun.'

The child psychologist allowed her apparent enthusiasm for

the subject to get the better of her and, leaning forward on to the desk, she elaborated further.

'There was a case many years ago,' she said, 'of a boy who was accused of doing it with a horse. He was condemned to death and then reprieved at the eleventh hour. Flintoff was his name and he looked after a mare for a coach owner, not far from West Ham, in a stable on Hackney Marshes. The coach driver followed Flintoff one morning into the stable and watched through a trap door in the hay loft. The coach driver swore on oath that he saw the boy get a bucket and put it behind the mare's heels before getting upon the pail and . . . He leaned over the mare with one hand forward on her back while the other supported her tail to one side. He was reprieved from the hangman when it was discovered that the principal witness, the coach driver, had not long been discharged from a madhouse . . .'

'That's what I mean,' I said, in desperation, 'you've got to be mad to do it or even think of doing it . . .'

'There are enough stories going round,' the psychologist interjected, 'to make it real, and not just stories about young boys; women in the Peruvian mountains going with apes, Gothic virgins with bears, Indian women with dogs. There are numerous stories of French shepherds husbanding their goats. Years ago, love of goats was epidemic in France. There was a case in Paris against a fellow named Jean Dupuy. He was sentenced to be guillotined and his dead body burned along with the goat. There was the case against a man named Saint-Jean de . . . something. He was found accomplishing the carnal act with a goat in the basement of the Hotel d'Auvergne, where he worked as a waiter. The chambermaid surprised him. She found him lying on the floor with the goat between his legs in the position that he wished to have it. Again, in France, at Chartres, there was a case where a . . .'

'It sounds as though the French like doing it?' I cut in.

'French, mad or indifferent, if they were caught they were punished. And if they didn't confess, they were tortured. There were two kinds of torture . . .'

'But if they were mad,' I interjected quickly, 'how could they be blamed?'

'Insanity,' she said, 'was a defence so long as the accused established that he was unable to comprehend the nature and consequences of the act. But, even here, the accused could only hope to lighten his sentence.'

Seemingly gratified by her outpouring, the child psychologist then asked me if I had any recollection of my father. 'Do you remember him at all? I mean your real father, not your stepfather.'

'I think he was one of my Mum's friends,' I replied.

'Well, I should hope so. Aren't you sure? Which friend? What was his name?'

'Fishy.'

'Is that a pet name your mother had for him?'

'That's his nickname.'

'Tell me about Fishy.'

'He's a window-cleaner,' I said. 'He used to clean our windows and he used to stay with us at the flat.'

'Tell me about the flat.'

All at once I recalled. 'The glass in the front door was smashed, near the keyhole. I don't know who broke it. It wasn't me. But it remained broken for the whole of my childhood. That's one pane of glass Fishy never had to clean and one that I wasn't responsible for smashing. Anybody could let themselves in without having to knock or use a key. Anybody.'

'Egypt, a prison without keys?'

'I don't know about that.'

'It was a first floor flat, wasn't it?'

'It was upstairs,' I said.

'No garden?'

I shook my head. 'The veranda overlooked the Memorial Ground, that was our garden, and the gravestones its furniture. The lavatory was next to the veranda and on the other side of the lavatory was a coal-cupboard. There was dust everywhere. You got to look like a miner. There was a cold-water tap by the window in the scullery and along the passage was the bathroom. If we wanted a hot bath we had to fill the bath up with hot water from the copper. It took ages.'

'Bit different from the children's home?'

'There was hot water at the children's home.'

'But apart from hot water, not much to recommend it?'

'Not much,' I said, peering out of the window.

The tops of the trees were luminous in the sunlight.

'Auntie Blodwen was always hitting us, especially if we were ill. Heaven help you if you were ill. She was disgusted by illness. Even when they found out that Ricky had leukaemia, she said it was a blessing, as though children in care may as well be dead anyway. His parents started coming to see him when they found out he was dying. He was glad to see them. He didn't know why they had suddenly started visiting and taking an interest. He thought his luck had changed for the better. How wrong can you get? After tea we used to play in the playroom or watch television in the office. And there was a garden with a silver birch and a sycamore. I could climb to the top of the silver birch. Every year I climbed a little higher. I used to stay up the tree for hours and nobody knew I was there. Sat on a thin branch, like a bird, wishing. I wished for bedtime. I looked forward to having the assurance of a blanket around my shoulders. But as much as I wanted to hide in bed, sometimes I would wake up and go down in the night, on my own or with Angela, Patricia, Barry, Trevor, George or Ricky, to raid the refrigerator.'

'It's a wonder Jenny didn't hear you and bark.'

'Of course she heard us, but we used to let her out of the playroom and she came with us. The refrigerator was in the larder, at the back of the scullery, a small, dark room with a hard, cold floor. We helped ourselves to whatever we wanted. It was scary sometimes because when we opened the door of the refrigerator a small light came on and threw shadows.'

'But you didn't do anything to Jenny?'

'No, I didn't. I came down in the night to feed the dog, not to fuck it.'

The child psychologist's questioning of me was interrupted as a man climbed the ladder that was leaning against the external sill of the closed window. He was an old man, I thought, at least forty-five, and he looked thin and puckered. He had a bucket of water in one hand and a chamois leather in the other. He started to clean the outside of the window. With a quiet professionalism he seemed not to notice me as he leaned back from his ladder to admire his work. Then he started to sing in a not too easy-going baritone with lots of vibrato.

I could hardly contain my surprise when I saw who it was and I turned to face the psychologist again. 'Do you believe what I've just told you?'

'I can tell when a person is telling the truth, Terry,' she said, without answering my question. 'Part of my job is to be able to do that.'

'Would you believe me if I told you the window-cleaner is my dad?'

She gave me a funny look, the sort of look that monkeys in

a zoo exhibit. She was leaning forward, motionless, and her eyes were searching.

'You have a choice, Terry,' she said. 'You can return to live with your mother and stepfather, but if you choose not to, another institution will be found for you to be sent to. But this time it will probably be a lot harsher. The people looking after you won't put up with any messing around. They'll be uncles, not aunties . . .'

I was excited, seeing Fishy, right there in front of me on the other side of the window. So close. 'He's my dad,' I said, interrupting her flow of words.

She reluctantly looked over her shoulder at Fishy. 'What makes you think the window-cleaner is your father?' she said, in desperation.

'I just *know* he is, that's all,' I said.

I had a sense of *déjà vu*. Somewhere at the back of my mind was a memory of Auntie Agnes asking me the very same question when Fishy came to clean the windows at Gibblings Shaw. *What makes you think the window-cleaner is your father?* I was in tears then. But now the tears couldn't get out. And anyway, my sadness was glossed over by the excitement of the moment.

The child psychologist was smiling now and shaking her head in disbelief.

'No,' I said. 'I mean it. The window-cleaner is my dad.'

Her smile broadened into a laugh.

I'd done it again.

'Come on, Terry,' she said. 'It's time to get serious. Do you want to go and live with your mother and stepfather?'

I needed somebody to take control and make everything OK, but instead I was being asked to make impossible decisions without even the time to think things through. I decided that the best alternative was to go and live with my mother and stepfather. I rationalised my decision by telling myself that I would have a degree of independence. I would have my own room where I could listen to my favourite music by myself, on a radio or a record-player, which I could save up for by doing a newspaper round or helping out on a milk float.

These were all-important considerations for a boy who was rapidly approaching his twelfth birthday. Despite having been abandoned by my mother, I was at least familiar with The Buildings. If I didn't return there, I didn't know where they might dump me. Better the devil you know. But I suppose the bottom line was that blood is thicker than water and, in spite of everything, I wanted to give *family* another chance.

20

The Buildings: Full Circle

I couldn't Adam and Eve it. The pane of glass was still missing from the front door, and, to boot, the square of plywood that had been nailed to the inside of the door frame to stop the draught along the passage had now disappeared.

I politely knocked. Without waiting for anybody to come, I reached inside and turned the knob of the Yale. I found my mother in the front room sitting at the piano contemplating the keys.

'You look like a ponce,' she said, standing up.

I stood in the doorway dressed in my school uniform with a solitary suitcase on the end of my arm. I put the suitcase down and removed my cap, respectfully.

She looked intently at me and seemed to notice immediately my softly washed hair, which before had been so greasy. She must have found my overall appearance and behaviour strange. She was dressed for The Buildings, a thin, sleeveless frock which exposed the hair under her armpits. It was a complete outfit with buttons all the way down the front from the neck to the knees. As I looked at her, she scratched under her arm.

The flat was still cluttered and dusty, everything was cheap, and there was still the smell of cooked food, alcohol and urine. Lampshades were conspicuously in short supply, and this as much as anything put the lid on any pretence at housewifery or house-husbandry.

She took me into the bedroom and I was presented to my stepfather, Joe, who was still lying in bed. Flat on his back, he said 'hello'. This was a culture shock to me now, presented to an adult who was lying in bed. He must have known I was coming. I know he only had one leg, but people with both legs missing have flown aeroplanes! Was it too much to expect him to get out of bed to greet me? Or was I affected by my stay in care and being uncharitable? Middle-class children aren't famous for entering into another's feelings. More to the point, had the LCC turned me into something middle class? Who was it inside that silly little school uniform with its pretty badge?

My half-sister, Rachel, let herself in through the front door carrying two babies – Martha crying in her arms, and the other unnamed and silent in her womb. Her other children came scurrying along the passage behind: Rookie, brandishing a toy gun; Melinda shouting at him; and Rachel's other daughter, Rosina, screaming at Melinda. They calmed down outside the bedroom door and together we stood and looked down at my stepfather as he lay in bed. He looked as though he belonged in a sideshow, lying there with a hollow in his face where his left eye was missing and the bedclothes unusually flat on one side of the bed because of the absence of a leg beneath.

I hadn't seen Rachel for six years, but I still felt something approaching affection for her. I don't know if my half-brotherly love was reciprocated. She was never free with her emotions.

I collected my suitcase from the end of the passage and was shown into my own bedroom. I found it bare except for the bed and a small cupboard. There was no wardrobe, but a couple of solid-looking wooden coat-hangers were hooked over the picture rail. The walls were hung with a patterned paper, but the corner behind the bed had not been finished and it looked scrappy. I put my suitcase down on the bare floorboards, and that's where it stayed with my spare clothes inside: several pairs of short trousers, long, gartered socks, and vests and pants which had been forwarded to Boyles Court from Gibblings Shaw.

It was uncalled for, but my mother then went into the front room and started to play the piano, in the same honky-tonk style that she had always played. I went back along the passage with Rachel and the children and we watched and listened. A lighted cigarette dangled from her mouth as her right hand played the melody in octaves and she tried to look flash. The left hand danced on the bass notes, first a single note, and then a chord several tones higher; a single note and then a chord, flowing left to right, a simple bass accompaniment under a melody.

Watching my mother, I was beginning to see that it was not so easy. Whichever way I looked at it, I could see that the left-hand pump was intricate and hard to get your fingers around. I hadn't recognised her outlandish talent until that moment.

Over and above the music was the noise of the children and I was expected to make a row with them. When I refused, it wasn't the children who admonished me, but the grown-ups. They thought there was something wrong with me; I was so quiet. Then suddenly they were all eating sweets and I took my share of these, suspecting rightly that this was my dinner.

The institutionalised order of the remand centre and the twisted symmetry of six long years in care were now replaced by this forgotten permissiveness. I filled my mouth with confectionery. The art of existing from one minute to the next had to be relearned, the ordeal of life resuffered in the old way.

In this traumatic state I enrolled the following day at my new secondary modern school, Pretoria – these days renamed as Eastlea. Rachel accompanied me and we went to meet the Headmaster in his office. He was friendly enough and he put me in 2B with Mr Talbot.

At this school the boys were segregated from the girls, as had been the case at my junior school. It was a long, narrow building and the girls' classrooms were at one end. The only time we got to see the girls, at a distance, was playtime, when they came out into their end of the playground. There was enmity between us as we lived up to our segregated status. I think it was about this time that I began to look on girls and all women with a degree of nervousness.

The boys at school would take the mickey out of my short trousers and gartered socks. That was bad enough, but there was no way I was going to go anywhere near the girls' end of the playground. To have the girls laughing at me too would have been too much to take. The other boys wore jeans, or at least long drainpipe trousers of some kind or other, and I was very much the odd one out.

Every morning as Mr Talbot came into the classroom he would ask: '2B or not 2B?' He would then take a register and we would commence our lessons. From the first day, I was hopelessly left behind. Worst of all, I knew I was still different. Walking home after school on my own, the other boys would follow me and taunt: 'Who wears short shorts?'

My mother, *desafinado* with many things, including the way young people behaved and dressed, simply said she could not afford them when I asked if I could have some long trousers. She had no idea how important it was for me to look the same as everybody else at school and to fit in visually, even if I couldn't compete academically.

The caring, understanding Rachel came to the rescue a day or two later and took me along to Rathebone Street market to buy a pair of jeans long enough to turn up at the bottom. The following Thursday she took me to a shoe shop in Stratford and I came out with a brand-new pair of winkle-pickers. It happened also to be my twelfth birthday, so her timing was perfect.

My new uniform was almost complete. All I needed now was the bicycle chain to go in my pocket. I still hated going to school. At least now it was just about bearable.

My relationship with my mother and stepfather went downhill fast. We had nothing in common and couldn't get along together at all. I would spend my evenings watching the television in the front room or mindlessly staring out of the window. I was so bored one evening that I actually found a hammer and nails and refitted the piece of plywood we used as a substitute for the missing pane of glass in the front door.

I remember on Sunday evenings I used to watch *Armchair Theatre* on the television. I don't know if it was aimed at children, but I used to enjoy it, and powerful images of some of the actors and actresses, Anthony Quayle, David McCullum, Gwen Watford and, of course, Harry H. Corbett, have remained with me after all this time.

After *Armchair Theatre* I would walk over to the railway and count the wagons of the goods trains. I would see the neighbours' children at a distance, talking together by the fence that separated the railway from the road, and want so much to go and join them and be one of them. I was much too shy and afraid of rejection to do that.

My mother and stepfather would sometimes send me on an errand to the off-licence to get some stout or brown ale, and I had to run the gauntlet of passing right in front of these teenagers, always on my guard, terrified they would say something nasty or even attack me physically.

When I returned home with the beer, my mother and stepfather would spend the evening sitting on the edge of their bed staring out of the window, drinking.

My stepfather kept a plastic bucket in the bedroom to urinate into at night because of the difficulty in getting along the passage to the toilet on his crutches. I could see the logic in this, but the stench of urine permeated the whole flat, night and day.

To try and put an end to it, when he was out I burned a hole in the bottom of the bucket. To make the hole I used the gadget for lighting the gas stove which shot out a nice long round flame. Sure enough, that night my stepfather urinated into the bucket and it went all over the floor. The next day the stench was worse than ever. I hoped I had made the point, but he simply went out and bought a new bucket. He had no authority and hardly ever spoke. When he wasn't at work or in the pub, he would make himself as comfortable as he could on the edge of his bed and look out of the window, drinking beer, whether my mother was with him or not. If anybody knocked at the front door he would not answer their knock, but leave them standing there until they became fed up with waiting and went away.

He didn't have an inkling of the needs of children or of how to bring up a family, and neither did my mother. And yet she had eight of us. When she dumped Fishy and married my stepfather, she took on a stepmother's responsibility for his three daughters, albeit they were older and not living at home. Nevertheless, all in all, my mother and stepfather were the parents of eleven children between them (those that I know of, that is).

At about this time my mother had a part-time job making tea in the canteen at the glassworks on the other side of the railway. It was night work and she would leave the flat as it became dark outside. I would watch her from the window making her way across the metal railway bridge, which we called the Peggy Leggy steps.

In the morning she would return across the Peggy Leggy

steps and come home with cigars in her bag for my stepfather and chocolate and sweets for me, gear that she'd stolen from the canteen.

It was a bad example to me, of course, and today if I can get away with something, a library book or not paying my train fare, I don't have too much of a conscience about it. I know dishonesty is wrong, but it's as if there's something from my past telling me that it's actually OK to get away with getting something for nothing providing one doesn't turn into a habitual wrongdoer and hardened criminal.

If ever my welfare officer knocked on the door unexpectedly, my mother was suddenly on her best behaviour and grovelling, 'Yerst, Mr King' and 'No, Mr King' in all the right places. He never stayed more than a few minutes and was unsympathetic; in fact, I know he disliked me intensely, maybe because I didn't conform to his middle-class perception of how children should behave. All he seemed to be intent on was teaching me social graces like saying, 'Very well, thank you, Mr King' when he asked me how I was.

I remember seeking permission from my mother one evening to go out on my bike (it had miraculously found its way from the children's home to The Buildings). She went into the bedroom and asked my stepfather if it would be OK. She was playing happy families, behaving as if my stepfather had some kind of headship. But he was such a weak character that I could see the question and the answer were pure pantomime.

I carried my bike down the stairs and cycled to the Century cinema in West Ham Lane (in the 1970s it was converted into a bingo hall, and later into a block of modern flats). I parked my bike and bunked into the pictures without paying. I had no money, but the film was X-rated anyway and they wouldn't have let a twelve-year-old in.

Bunking in was easy. If you pushed an exit door in the right place, then the bar behind the door would rise up enough to get the door open. Alternatively, you could stand there until somebody came out and then nip in quickly before the door closed again. This wasn't the first time I'd bunked in without paying, and as usual I manipulated one of the doors and opened it a few inches. It was pitch-black in there, but there was no sound; this was obviously a part of the film where there was no dialogue or music (maybe some monster or homicidal maniac was just twitching silently). I was excited as I opened the door further and stepped forward. Suddenly I was being hit on the back of the head repeatedly with something heavy.

I was used to seeing pictures in comic strips of brightly coloured stars rotating around the heads of characters that are being hit or punched, but I never imagined the stars were real. I was falling, and came to rest on top of a heap of something that was not soft, but at least yielding. It was a pile of coal. The door I had mistakenly gone through did not lead into the cinema. It opened over a shaft which lent access to the cinema's coal-cellar. The pile of coal undoubtedly saved me from serious injury.

Dazed, I picked myself up and groped around in the darkness, stupidly still intent on finding a seat and watching a film. Instead my hands came into contact with a metal ladder that was bolted to the side of the shaft. I came to my senses and slowly climbed back up towards the door above me, each rung of the ladder representing one of the clouts to the back of the head that I had received as I fell.

I reached the top of the shaft, scrambled out, and got on my bike. My hair and my clothes were full of coal dust and my body bruised.

Outside West Ham Underground station I was stopped by some youths. I vaguely recognised them. They were local girls and boys and they knew me to look at. I must have looked so strange, sitting there on my bike without lights, covered in something black, and the shock of what had happened showing in my face. I was too much of an easy target for them. They pushed me off my bike and started kicking and punching me as I lay in the road. I suppose these children too had suffered beatings at the hands of others, and they were simply letting out their pent-up feelings on a soft target.

When I got home and my mother opened the door, I don't know what I must have looked like.

'What happened? What happened?' she screamed in my ear.

I wheeled my bike along the passage to my bedroom and tentatively pushed the door open.

I sat on my bed and looked out of the window. There were no tears. But I did wonder if there was anywhere I could go that was safe and welcoming.

I still needed to run. I was born to. I must either go away once and for all or remain superfluous for ever. I must escape and hide. I was too painfully aware that this council flat was not the place to lick my wounds. I decided to leave in the morning and started to formulate a plan in the back of my mind.

I was afraid of being alone in my bedroom in the dark. (The light bulb had gone several days previously and there wasn't one to replace it. When I asked my mother for a replacement, she had complained about the expense and shouted at me about the high cost of electricity.)

After my mother and stepfather had gone into the bedroom with a drink, I stayed up late thinking, and watching the television in the front room on my own until the epilogue. Watching the television didn't inspire or reassure me at all because I found some of the programmes – *The Invisible Man*, for example – really frightening, but there was nothing else for me to do, except look out of the window. And then when I eventually went to bed I was even more afraid and confused. There were no curtains in my bedroom and the street lighting threw shadows on the walls. And I heard noises in the cupboard.

I eventually dropped off to sleep and wet the bed. This gave rise to more resentment from my mother the following morning.

Southend-on-Sea seemed as good a place as any to run away to. It was a popular resort town, easily accessible from the East End of London, and of course I'd been fostered there – albeit only for a day.

Instead of going to school on Monday morning I took the train and, during the ticketless ride, I resolved to get a job in an amusement arcade or at a funfair or even on the pier. I was only twelve years old, but I looked older. They must need people for all sorts of things, I convinced myself.

When I arrived the summer season was underway and I felt good. The arcades were open and the holidaymakers were enjoying themselves eating and drinking and spending money on the rides. I walked up and down the arcades and stopped to buy myself something to eat with the couple of shillings I had in my pocket.

But little by little, as the morning wore on, I became disillusioned. I honestly couldn't see how I was going to get a job. I didn't have the courage to go up to somebody and ask for work. What would you say? 'I need a job'? 'Do you happen to have a vacancy for a homeless twelve-year-old?' 'I'll do anything'?

I spent the afternoon walking up and down the pier, and after that there was nothing else to do and nowhere to go. The hours dragged by and I felt enormously sad. My hopes had come to nothing.

As the light faded and the wind started to come in from the sea, I borrowed a deckchair from the beach and took it with me into the cover of some trees that grew above the esplanade. I sat down uncomfortably in the middle of the trees and looked at my watch. It was only nine o'clock. I envisaged the long night ahead of me and an unwished-for tomorrow, walking up and down the longest pier in the world.

I don't think I have ever felt so lonely in my life and at last the tears came. I was unable to hold them back any longer.

I woke up feeling dirty and aching. I took the train back to London and spent the day wandering around Liverpool Street.

As evening approached I made my way back to the East End and my mother's council flat as if drawn there by an invisible thread. There was nowhere else I could go and I stood outside for ages, too proud and embarrassed after running away to knock on the door and ask if they would have me back.

I turned away and walked the streets for hours before being drawn back by this thread of need. It was the middle of the night when I finally climbed the drainpipe to the veranda at the rear of The Building and, with sand in my face, went in through the open lavatory window.

Letting myself down on to the lavatory seat I heard my mother, as she lay in bed, say to my stepfather that there was somebody breaking in.

I sidestepped into the coal-cupboard and made even more of a racket as the heap of coal yielded to every move I made. Then I heard my stepfather, still in bed, deny that he could hear a thing and I felt that he was such a coward. What if I'd been a real burglar or, worse, a homicidal maniac? Wouldn't my stepfather have done anything to protect my mother? I went along the passage and into my bedroom and lay down on the bed, disgusted. I very quickly fell asleep on top of the bed, fully dressed in my blazer, turned-up jeans and winkle-pickers.

I suppose my mother had had to report me missing to the police when I ran away, and now that I was back she would have had no choice but to inform them of that fact also. Of course she knew it was me entering through the lavatory window during the night, and once I was asleep she had slipped out and telephoned the police from the telephone box in Manor Road.

I was woken by the perennial policeman standing over me. 'Wake up, sonny. Come on. Come with me.'

My mother was hovering in the doorway in an agitated state. I sidled past her into the passage and then went into the scullery and, taking the comb from the top pocket of my school blazer, combed my hair in front of the small wall mirror.

The policeman waited patiently by the door and I remember that as I watched his reflection in the mirror, his expression and stance revealed to me that he had grasped the sheer pathos of what was going on. My predicament was pathetic and he knew it.

I put my cherished comb back into my top pocket behind my silly little school badge and, without saying goodbye to my mother, I went with the policeman to the waiting police car.

21

Brand New Bag

*Heavenly Father, please show our family what
we need to do in order to be happy.*

This short prayer is the outcome of a suffocated childhood. For a fatherless child from West Ham who failed his eleven-plus, there was no real hope of anything beyond childhood for me other than a factory floor or the cavernous subterranean abode of a public lavatory. Deprived of access to further education, in spite of the political will that was around at the time, Tate & Lyle's sugar refinery in Silvertown, the glassworks on the other side of the Peggy Leggy steps, or Dagenham Motors provided the only alternative to following in my stepfather's footsteps and becoming a council worker. A public lavatory could for me have been the end of life's journey.

But my ambition could not be thwarted by an accident of birth. I longed too much for something different. The less likely it seemed that any future lay in store for me, and the more numerous the enemy telling me to face up to life and get myself down to Tate & Lyle's, then the more brightly burned this lamp of hope that refused to be extinguished.

When I returned from Southend I was driven in the police car back to Boyles Court, the remand centre in Brentwood. I subsequently appeared before a juvenile court in Stratford in East London and was sent to an Approved School for a period of three years. Shortly before my fifteenth birthday they released me on licence, and that was the end of my education. No prizes for guessing where my brains were or where I went to live. I returned to The Buildings to live with my mother and stepfather, and I was sent to work, not at Tate & Lyle's sugar refinery in Canning Town, nor the glassworks or Dagenham Motors, but to the Jaffa furniture factory in Manbey Grove, Stratford.

I fell into a routine of getting up early, working hard all day at the factory, and coming home knackered to sit in front of the television until bedtime. I had no friends and on Saturdays I would lie in bed at least until midday, and the best part of Sunday was spent reading the *News of the World*, which was still my mother's and stepfather's preferred 'linen' and always to hand.

Things started to change when walking home from work one day I saw the rag-and-bone man and noticed the head and neck of a guitar sticking out from the depths of his barrow. Perhaps it was the memory of my mother handing over my pedal car to him all those years before, when I was six, that made me want to claw something back; or maybe it was just the sad look of the instrument as it lay prostrate beneath a heap of junk. Whatever it was, I made a snap decision.

'How much do you want for that guitar?' I called across the road as we drew level.

''alf a dollar,' the rag-and-bone man replied.

'Half a dollar' was the amount he had paid my mother for the car. I crossed the road and handed over 2/6d. He gave the guitar to me and as we wandered off in opposite directions, looking back over my shoulder I couldn't help thinking that the rag-and-bone man's gait was remarkably similar to my own.

During the coming week I replaced the missing strings, spent hours trying to tune it this way and that, and tried to call to mind the chords I had learnt at junior school. On Saturday I slept as usual, and on Sunday, after my stepfather's curiosity was satiated, I read the *News of the World*. This particular week, on the penultimate page something caught my eye:

PLAY IN A DAY

WITH BERT WEEDON

It was a serialised guitar course for absolute beginners. There were some chord shapes set out in tablature; there were words to a song, and above the words was the chord symbol so you knew exactly when to change the position of your fingers. Even before I'd fetched my guitar from the bedroom, it seemed I couldn't go wrong.

I had seen Bert Weedon on Bruce Forsyth's *Sunday Night at the London Palladium* and ARTV's *Lucky Dip*, so I thought this might be worth looking into. Fascinated, I looked again at the newspaper and the first lesson and, following Bert's straightforward instructions, I brought the guitar to life. I felt an immediate sense of achievement, and from that moment on I wanted to learn everything there was to learn about the instrument and to play it as often and as well as I could. I was starting out on the bottom rung, but that was an advantage because it meant I had everything to gain and nothing to lose. I could reach for the stars without the fear of failure getting in the way.

Soon after, without the burden of love to shoulder, I spread my wings. Neglecting to inform my mother, I left The Buildings for good; this time I didn't run, I walked. I was no longer being chased by the police or shepherded by social workers and court officials. I was free of them.

I rented a room at 1 Crosby Road, Forest Gate. The room, at the back of the house, was cold and damp with only a bed and a wardrobe for furniture. It was neither better nor worse than The Buildings. The wallpaper was peeling and the carpet so filthy that I would have been better off without it. Unpleasant smells wafted along the passage from a shared kitchen and bathroom, but I wasn't to be discouraged. I stuffed an old sock against the bridge of my guitar to dampen the strings and practised like there was no tomorrow.

I then started going to what used to be called 'night school' one evening a week for guitar lessons. The lessons were held at a school in Poplar, off the East India Dock Road. The teacher's name was Stewart Bellamy. He played with the Edmundo Ross orchestra, but also worked as a pit musician in West End theatres and would stop off at the school on his way in to work from the leafy suburb of Romford. He was working at the Adelphi at the time where the musical *Charlie Girl* was showing, starring Joe Brown and Dame Anna Neagle.

Be that as it may, Stewart boasted to the class one night that he had had lessons from Bert Weedon. So impressed was I by this that I asked Stewart if he gave private lessons himself. I had come to night school straight from work and my hair was full of sawdust. My clothes were dirty and my hands in no fit state to hold a musical instrument. And when I tapped on the parquet floor in time to the music it was with a pair of enormous hobnailed boots on the end of my feet. Stewart looked down at me, his black bow-tie already in place around his neck ready for his theatre gig. I was seated behind a desk, guitar balanced on my knee, looking up, waiting for an answer to my question. After a momentary hesitation he said 'yes' and he laid down his terms and conditions: £1.2s.6d an hour to be paid a week in advance, and I must always arrive for my lesson at least five minutes early, or else! I returned to my bedsit that night as happy as Larry.

The following morning in the communal kitchen I bumped into Pamela, the girl who rented a room at the front of the house. She was preparing something for breakfast and offered to share it with me. I swallowed hard, accepted, and before I knew it I was sitting on her bed eating cornflakes. Pamela was a couple of years older than me and she explained that she was a single parent. She had had sex only once, she insisted, after getting drunk at a party.

Her baby was being looked after by a friend because our landlady didn't allow children, and anyway Pamela had to work – at Lesney's Matchbox Toys factory during the day and as a barmaid at night.

One thing led to another and before the month was out I gave up my own room at the other end of the passage and moved in with Pamela. I also gave up my day job and did the odd night's casual work at Johnson's Bakery in Abberton Walk instead. Johnson's were always looking for people to load up the vans with their quota of bread and cakes, and we casual labourers collected our money the following morning at the end of the shift, in cash, no questions asked.

Moving in with Pamela was a mistake because when we irretrievably fell out over me giving up my day job, she gave me my marching orders and I found myself outside on the pavement, guitar in one hand, amplifier in the other. I had an electric guitar by this time and a driving licence. I placed my guitar and amp in the back of a clapped-out blue mini van that I had recently bought from a local secondhand car dealer. The van had originally belonged to a brewery apparently, because it had Inde Coope written all over it. I sat down in the driver's seat contemplatively, and then in a daze drove off into the night.

With no money and nowhere to go, I was forced to sleep in the van and make it my home. When I went for my guitar lesson at Stewart's house that week, I explained to him what had happened. He thought for a moment and then said: 'The bass player at Quaglino's has rooms to let. Give him a ring.'

Stewart gave me the number and after my lesson I drove round and round until I found a red call-box that was in working order. I dialled and explained that I had been given this number by Stewart Bellamy.

There was nothing available immediately, but a room was being done up and would be ready in a couple of weeks. 'Why not come round before then,' the friendly voice on the other end of the line said, 'to see if it will be suitable? How is Stewart?'

The following morning I stopped my van at a public lavatory for a wash and brush-up and then, by appointment, made my way to the bass-player-at-Quaglino's house, which turned out to be in Romford Road, Forest Gate, uncomfortably close to my old lodgings!

Answering my knock, the bass player/landlord shook hands with me formally, introduced himself as Bernie Woods, and took me immediately along the corridor to the room in question, the middle room downstairs. The first thing I noticed was the coin-box telephone on the wall outside the room, and I imagined living in this house with the benefit of no longer having to drive halfway across London to find a call-box that worked every time I wanted to ring somebody.

There were no major renovations taking place. The room was simply being redecorated, but even like this it was a hundred times better than the premises I had recently moved out of in Crosby Road. When I told Bernie that I was homeless and living in a mini van, he was speechless. And then I asked him how much the rent was.

After a moment of quiet he suggested I should take the room immediately and the work would be completed around me, so to speak. 'In fact,' Bernie continued, 'if you finish the work your-self, you can have the room rent free for a while.' He stepped outside into the hall and pointed to where the bathroom was and then explained who lived in the other rooms of the house. 'My own flat is that one,' he said, pointing to the end of the corridor. 'Come on, I'll put the kettle on. Are you any *good* at painting?'

In the coming days, with tools and materials that were provided, I painted the woodwork, papered the walls, and carpeted the floor. One by one I was introduced to the other tenants: Martin – I'm not sure what Martin did for a living, but he occupied the front room downstairs and had a girlfriend called Yvonne; David was a shipping clerk who had the front room upstairs; Hazel, a student, had the middle room upstairs above my room; and Salam, also a student, had the end flat upstairs. We all shared many cups of coffee together and none of our doors was ever locked. There was a sense of community, something quite new to me. Surrounded by all these friends that I knew I could trust, I felt secure at last. I slowly started to find work with the guitar, mostly pub gigs to begin with, locally in the East End, poorly paid, but the experience was priceless. I also felt confident enough to enrol at Waltham Forest Technical College for a graded theory of music course. I attended the college one evening a week to follow a Royal Schools of Music exam syllabus.

Stewart Bellamy took me along to the Adelphi one afternoon for a matinée performance so I could look over his shoulder at the guitar score as he performed in the pit. While the band played, Joe Brown, Dame Anna Neagle, Derek Nimmo and others cavorted behind us on stage in their underwear – it was all part of the script!

In the coming months I continued to be Stewart's unofficial understudy, and I kept up my studies for the theory of music exam at Waltham Forest Tech. I began to soar like an eagle and gleaned what I could until an apprenticeship was served. As summer approached I was offered a job with a band at a holiday camp and jumped at the chance. It was at Warners in Sheerness, Essex; they needed a guitar player for the summer season.

A day or two before I left for Sheerness I received the result of my theory of music exam in the afternoon post. Bernie and Salam were also at home when the letter landed on the carpet and, making their way to the front door, neither of them was in any doubt as to its contents. Crouching down, I picked up the envelope like a thief in the night and took it with me into my room. Bernie and Salam followed behind.

I paced from one side of the room to the other. I knew that the maximum number of marks for the examination was 99 out of a hundred, but I couldn't bear to look and find out how few of those 99 marks I had been awarded.

'Well, open it,' Salam said.

'No, I can't,' I answered.

'Go on,' Bernie said, 'open the envelope.'

'No, I can't,' I said. 'I've never passed an exam in my life.'

'Maybe you *have* passed an exam,' Bernie said, 'but you won't know if you don't open the envelope.'

'We haven't got all day,' Salam said. '*Open* the envelope.'

I could stall no longer, so I prised the envelope open with my thumb. I couldn't believe my eyes: I had obtained the maximum 99 marks. I showed the result to the others. Bernie and Salam both looked at one another, and then together they patted me on the back.

'What about you?' I said to Salam. 'Have you received your results yet?'

'They came this morning,' he said. 'I did extremely well. Not quite as well as you, though.'

'Phew!' I exclaimed, as I put the kettle on.

My appetite for learning had been awakened, and later I would do further music grades, tackle other subjects, and blossom academically, claiming for myself at last the intellectual stimulation and excitement that perhaps had always been my rightful inheritance. But for the time being it was enough to know that I could do it, and I departed for Sheerness, continuing to rent the room in Forest Gate while I was away.

When I returned to London, Bernie introduced me to Len Walker, a guitar player who worked with the BBC Radio Orchestra. I started going to Len Walker's house in Cricklewood once a week and we practised sight-reading together using violin studies for material (the violin has a range similar to the guitar). Len told me much later that I used to frighten the life out of him, because he had to struggle so hard to keep up with me!

I remember we were practising together once when the phone rang. It was James Brown, the soul singer, on the line needing to speak to Len. He was over from America to record and was phoning round booking musicians, for sessions – musicians who had a feel for the kind of music he wanted to produce. This was after 'Papa's Got a Brand New Bag' and James Brown was refining his style. I was mightily impressed.

I was also helped by Sid Jacobson. He was a phenomenal guitar player who sometimes used to come to the house at 289 Romford Road to go over things with Bernie when they had a recording session or broadcast looming. Bernie introduced me to Sid, and he was only too glad to show me various riffs. Sometimes we would all meet up at Ronnie Scott's in Frith Street.

After my very first visit to Ronnie Scott's, I was hooked, and returned regularly to listen to Barney Kessel, John Williams, and many other great guitar players and jazz singers. I always sat right at the front, stayed late, and caught a night bus home, if I was lucky.

Christmas came and went, and one day Len Walker phoned to say that he'd heard that British Transport Hotels were looking for a guitar player to join a band at the famous and historic five-star Gleneagles Hotel in Scotland and he wondered if I was interested. *Was I interested?!* I wrote to apply for the job immediately. There was no audition, but an interview instead, at the Piccadilly Hotel in London. I duly went along, more than a little nervous, and had tea in the lounge with a musical director called Joe Orlando. He told me that Gleneagles would be opening again in March, that it was a long season, and the orchestra would be expected to play every night (in other words, no night off).

I did two summer seasons at Gleneagles, then I moved to Weybridge in Surrey and continued to follow my chosen career as a jobbing guitar player – not exactly a pop star, but living where I was on Saint George's Hill, nesting in the company of one or two. The chance of a flat had come up and it had been too good to miss. I had also begun to feel a little claustrophobic in London and it felt good to be living in the countryside.

I subsequently bought a plot of land in France and moved here, having finally made up my mind that I preferred the sticks to the big smoke. I met my wife within a few hours of arriving. *Comme si nous étions destinés à nous rencontrer*! She is everything to me and we have built a house together, with strong foundations.

Epilogue

I have enjoyed writing this book and feel stronger for having done so. Perhaps I could write a book now about living in Weybridge or France. What would be the more compelling, I wonder? Or maybe I could write on a different subject altogether. One way or another I would really love to have the opportunity to continue writing.

First, though, there are jobs crying out to be done around the house. And there's my guitar gently weeping in the corner – a friend I might neglect from time to time, but one I will never disown.

Why did I choose the guitar as the medium for my music? To begin with, my choice was limited. Living, as I did, in Manor Road Buildings, West Ham, I could not have chosen the violin. If anybody had seen me playing a violin or even carrying one around, at best I would have been laughed at – and at worst I would have had my face kicked in for being a drip! For the same reason, I could not have chosen the viola, the 'cello, the piccolo or double bassoon. A bass guitar might have been approved of, but I myself believed even then, without realising it, that bass is for fundamentalists.

The guitar, on the other hand, was liberating, vibrant, popular, safe and street cred-worthy. Choosing the guitar was rather like an arranged marriage, it wasn't really a choice. It was an alliance of necessity. Having said that, many arranged marriages are hugely successful and I have come to respect and love the instrument over the years. I also chose the guitar as my first instrument because it is a lead instrument, and I needed not only to express myself, but to assert myself as well, having been oppressed and suppressed for so long as a child and a teenager. I needed to push myself forward, into the front line. I think there was, and still is, a bit of the actor in me and I had a strong urge to take up the position of centre stage. I chose the guitar, then, for the same reason that shy people choose to be actors or comedians.

But there's also something about a vibrating string that turns me on. I like the sound, but I also like the feel of the strings beneath my fingers. I like woodwind instruments, too, especially the oboe, which can sometimes sound like a string vibrating to my way of hearing. There is a special something about the sound of a string vibrating.

It would be remiss of me not to disclose to the initiated which guitars and amps I use. I've always used a Strat and I still love the sound of the middle pick-up. I've parted with one or two really nice guitars over the years. One should never do that. I regret it now. I still have a (valve) Twin Reverb, which is the Rolls-Royce of amplifiers as far as I'm concerned. The sound is so rich and creamy and there's so much body. I've never heard anything like it – in fact, I don't hear it, I *feel* it.

I know I'm spoilt! I use an American sound system for vocals and saw exactly the same kind of microphone as mine being used by a judge at the Old Bailey a few years back, so I reckon it must be OK. All this gear is of pensionable age, but it produces the sound I want so I'm happy to go on using it.

I still ask myself why I felt the need to put pen to paper like this. Being a published author of course is a romantic concept in itself, and I've been aware from page one that I might be looking for some unwholesome celebrity. But as I have forged ahead with my story I have come to realise that the need to *share* my experiences with you is the more legitimate reason for writing. I now feel a sense of relief and disburdenment, and can at last leave the misery behind and get on with fulfilling my dreams with more *joie de vivre* than ever.

As Basil Fawlty would say: 'Oh! I'm so happy' (in the *Fawlty Towers* episode called 'A Touch of Class'). The difference between me and poor old Basil is that I mean it. I live with my wife and daughter beside a lake in a conservation area halfway down a narrow country lane with a No Entry sign at the top which means we hardly ever see any traffic. The house is set in three acres with pine, poplar, apple, walnut and quince trees, and we have a stream running between them that eventually winds its way down to the Vézère. The stream supports freshwater crayfish and gudgeon and attracts all manner of wildlife including badgers, a pair of herons – who like it so much they are more or less resident – and squirrels that come down from the trees to drink at dusk. I can see them now as I look out through my open study window. Sometimes deer will come up to the house to have a look and see what's going on. Red foxes are more common still and it's quite a sight to see them racing across the land. If you've ever watched this, you will know what I mean. Oh, and next door we have a herd of cows.

We have two dogs of our own, Margaret, a German Pointer, and Cachou, who is small and lively with black curly hair, but of uncertain genesis. We also have a cat called Maggie, three goldfish, and two sheep to help keep the grass down – whose joint name is Dagenham Motors because they are always on strike (pronounced *D'Agenham Mowers*)! They sit under the table in the garden all day shading themselves from the sun. I've told them: 'If you don't come out from under that table you're gonna end up on top of it as mutton.' But they just give me sheepish looks and refuse to budge. All around us friendly French farmers grow their crops, and something of whatever is in season is always left outside our front door.

I feel so blessed, but I never forget that once upon a time, because of adverse domestic circumstances, I could have been destined for a life of crime. I'm grateful to the people who have helped me, and that includes you for reading my book. I'm also grateful to Stewart Bellamy, Len Walker, Bert Weedon (for *Play in a Day*) and Bernie Woods especially, but also Martin Beake, Yvonne Lowe, Salam Salam (whose first name really is the same as his second), and David Goodwin and Hazel Dunkley. David and Hazel married one another and moved into one room, and are still together more than thirty years later. They have two sons, now grown up, that any parent would be tremendously proud of. They also reside in less-cramped accommodation these days, having bought a house and moved out to a leafy suburb.

I held my hand out to them and they took it. It wasn't the Church, social workers or governments that spun me around and turned me into something; it was a small circle of friends who had no time for 'pretend do-gooding'. Perhaps as much as anything it was music itself that saved me. I recommend it to you, from Snoop Dogg to Tchaikovsky: hear it, write it, make it, download it and play it. It's a sacrament in its own right, a means of grace.

Religion featured heavily during my years in care and some aspects still weigh on me, but I don't belong to a church and I don't call myself a Christian. Prayer is not the first thing that enters my mind when I wake up in the morning; rather, I think of my stomach and what I'm going to have for breakfast! During my childhood I went to bed with myths, but also with nightmares, having been touched by the problems and insecurities of the real world. In my dreams, North Woodford's suburban hymns of praise sounded hypocritical, the Easter anthems came across as sanctimonious, and I could hear beyond the singing voices. I heard status being worshipped by members of a church which, at its origins, I now know had been anything but middle class. When I prayed it was by rote, and when they sent me back to the real world and washed their hands of me, they wounded for ever any feeling I might have had for an anthropomorphic God.

'I Believe in God the Father Almighty, Maker of heaven and earth: And in . . .' and that's as far as I've been able to go since. I was cut off from the Church halfway through a creed. Myth ended in Sir Winston Churchill's constituency and reality began in the inner city. I did not reject God or the Church and its cucumber-sandwiches-with-the-crusts-cut-off ministers. I was excommunicated before my first communion, prior to having had time to rebel. It was a sudden break and, confused as I was by churchmen who told me dogs do not go to heaven and aunties who assured me they did, I'm happy to be out of it, and glad nobody came looking.

Today my religion is Bourgeois Liberalism, which means I'm an open-minded materialist. It's not as bad as it sounds and it doesn't mean I don't believe.

My three half-brothers, four half-sisters and three stepsisters have over thirty grown-up children between them. The majority of them live in council flats in deprived areas of London and are heavily reliant on the state for every penny. I know of only one member of my family, including my extended family, who has been redeemed in the same way as I have. One of Rachel's grandchildren managed to get to university, graduated, and is now Head of the Special Needs department at a school in South

Epilogue

London. My daughter, named Emily after her grandmother, is doing really well at school and has been moved up a year above her age group, something we are allowed to do in France. We have a piano at home in our front room and young Emily is learning to play, properly.

I visited my mother recently, just before she died. I took the flight from Bergerac to Stansted and then the District Line to West Ham. It was over thirty years since I had seen her or had any kind of contact whatsoever. She was very old and frail and, although her mind was sound, there were moments when she seemed not to remember me. I asked her who my father was, but she didn't answer. She just laughed, abusing me till the end.

Endnote

In 1957 Elvis Presley simulated sex on stage at a Los Angeles concert with a toy dog, the crowd went wild, and television pictures of the event were screened around the world. The news clip that caught Auntie Blodwen's eye in the office of Gibblings Shaw that day when Fishy came to clean the windows may well have been from this concert, and might have given rise to her obsessive idea that one of the children at the home was having sex with the Irish setter.

Acknowledgements

To my publisher, Judith Longman, for your commitment, editorial advice, support and encouragement, thank you. Cecilia Moore and Linda Crosby edited the book with skill and patience. To Patrick Knowles, Elizabeth Ward and the rest of the team at Hodder & Stoughton, thank you for helping to make a dream come true! To my agent, Sheila Ableman and to Jacky Trevane, a special *Merci*! Dave and Anne Hale, Michael Taylor and Irina Zarb read some early essays of mine and encouraged me to continue writing. Geoff Sanders and Rita Angell helped with research, Richard Durack and Jenni Munroe at Archives and Local Studies, Stratford Library, London E15, provided two invaluable photographs. My grateful thanks go out to you all. To my wife Nadine and my daughter Emily, for your love, patience, kindness, goodness, gentleness, self-control, and for the joy and peace you bring me, God's Richest Blessings. And thank *you* for reading this book and making it all worthwile.

Terry